REFRAMING RELIGIOUS LIFE

DIARMUID O'MURCHU MSC

Reframing
Religious Life

An expanded vision for the future

ST PAULS

ST PAULS
Morpeth Terrace, London SW1P 1EP, United Kingdom
Moyglare Road, Maynooth, Co. Kildare, Ireland

© ST PAULS (UK) 1998

First published 1998.

ISBN 085439 543 1

Set by TuKan, High Wycombe

Printed by The Guernsey Press Co. Ltd, Guernsey, C.I.

ST PAULS is an activity of the priests and brothers of the
Society of St Paul who proclaim the Gospel through the media
of social communication

With love and gratitude
I dedicate this book to
Elizabeth Smyth RC
whose engagement with life
amid joy and suffering
has led many people
to prophetic and liminal places

Contents

Preface

The first edition of this book appeared in January 1995, some two months after the 1994 Synod on religious life. The final chapter offered some reflections on both the process leading up to the Synod, and the deliberations which ensued from the Synod itself. The final document of the Synod did not appear until 1996, by which stage the Synod event itself felt like a long distant memory.

Now in 1998, the Synod is virtually a non-event in the contemporary history of Religious Life. It has had little or no impact in helping us to understand what's happening in religious life today, nor in offering a realistic hope for the future. Consequently, and not without due consideration, I have decided to leave aside the chapter on the 1994 Synod. I have replaced it with a Chapter on *Spirituality*. There are two main reasons for this choice. Our world is engulfed with a new spiritual hunger. It is not readily apparent within the major religions or in the formal churches. It belongs much more to the 'cutting edge' where people explore questions of meaning and pursue the search for more wholesome living.

I believe that we, religious, more than anybody else, are called to encounter this new spiritual ferment with that wisdom and compassion that belongs to our liminal vocation. We carry in our hearts the heritage of the liminal margins, and the prophetic call to stand apart with those who seek new hope.

However, we cannot make this quality of response, unless we ourselves are imbued with a spirituality that can embrace the liminal call with all its challenges and paradoxes. This is my second main reason for the choice of spirituality. The spiritual traditions of our recent past, and the underlying spiritual vision of the entire patriarchal era (of some 10,000 years) is largely irrelevant – and in fact, often debilitating – in addressing the engagements of this new spiritual moment.

With the addition of this extra chapter, and other minor modifications made throughout the text, the call to conceptualise anew (reframe) what the vowed life is about takes on greater depth and clearer application. To stand before the reality of our world today – especially at the creative margins of suffering and hope – requires the contemplative gaze and intuitive vision of the living Spirit. To see how things really connect – and how the forces of patriarchy fragment and disconnect – is the wisdom our world hungers for. It is in reclaiming our world once more as the fertile soil for the witness of religious life that we, too, will be born anew.

Introduction

*To live in an evolutionary spirit means to engage
with full ambition and without any reserve in the
structure of the present, and yet to let go and flow
into a new future when the right time has come.*

                                              Erich Jantsch

Reframing is a concept used in systems theory and in one
of its better known applications, family therapy. It invokes
a new configuration or a series of different configurations
which offer fresh options for understanding a system's
mode of operation. By exploring fresh movement among
individual elements (e.g. members of a family), the whole
system can alter significantly. If the sullen withdrawn daughter is invited and allowed to voice her protest (instead of
sublimating or repressing it), not only does her role change
within the system but the entire repertoire of family interaction is likely to undergo modification.

   Watzlawick and Alia (1974) describe it as 'the gentle art
of reframing'. It is a liberating process, inviting us to
examine and hopefully outgrow staid and rigid ways of
being. Obviously the larger and more complex the system,
the more difficult will be the task of reframing because
more resistances are embedded in the system itself. And if
structures are validated by a prolonged historical existence,
and buttressed by powerful religious and emotional ideologies, then the task of reframing may be quite daunting.

   On the other hand we tend to underestimate the fragility
of 'powerful' systems. It is often at a point of extreme and
prolonged rigidity that a system is close to collapse. The
creative energies are exhausted; the will to life is all but
usurped; the pain of imminent extinction is so real that
nobody dares to acknowledge it. Many institutions in our

11

world today – political, social, economic and ecclesiastical – are utterly exhausted; inertia, despondency, co-dependency and denial abound. In many such cases reframing may not be possible until the old edifice crumbles and dies. Then all things become possible once more.

Our self-understanding

Religious life is a dominant ecclesiastical institution of the western world. Even in the southern hemisphere most forms of the vowed life are Eurocentric, embedded in structural formalities inherited from the West although many orders and congregations in the West no longer adhere to these mores. As a dominant institution religious life within the Church is relegated to the status of special consecration, so that religious may be agents for evangelisation (see John Paul II 1996). What all this means in practice is perceived very differently in the various sectors of religious life. There is in fact very little congruity between the expectations of the official Church and those of the rank and file in our orders and congregations. Among religious themselves there is an enormous range of self-understanding – or lack of it – pertaining to role and purpose.

In the eyes of the general public in the West religious tend to be perceived as specialists in outstanding service especially in education, hospital work and ministry to the marginalized of society. The general public perceive Religious in terms of *function* (role), not in terms of *consecration*. In the great eastern traditions of Hinduism, Buddhism and some Christian variants of these Religious are considered to be 'people set apart', whose task is never clearly defined, but intuitively is understood to affect the quality of cultural life for a wide range of people. (This role I describe as *liminal* and its meaning is explored in chapter three.)

Like many western systems of our time, religious life is in crisis, dwindling in numbers and in cultural impact, unsure of its purpose, confused about its role and quite ambivalent about its future. In fact its future is not in doubt, as many historians of religious life highlight. What is in doubt is the survival of the present model (framework) of the vowed life. There is in fact no one current model but there does exist a dominant stereotype with many of the characteristics of post-Reformation spirituality and theology: *patriarchal* (dominated by masculine values and a hierarchical power structure); *dualistic* (soul v. body earth v. heaven, perfect v. sinful); *legalistic* (salvation by the observance of law); *Jansenistic* (derogatory of the created worldly order); *Eurocentric* (Christian religious life is superior to other [pagan] forms).

Dying and letting go

The renewal of religious life advocated by the Second Vatican Council and promulgated in its documents *Lumen Gentium* (chapter six) and *Perfectae Caritatis* helped to shake up a staid, conformist system. The shaking up actually exacerbated the disintegration that was already taking place; for many among us the fragmentation became apparent for the first time. The dismantling process now seems irreversible – a process all too familiar to historians of religious life. We are undergoing a classic paschal journey of death and resurrection. As the seed falls into the ground and dies, so in due course there will spring forth sprouts of new life, fresh hope and novel possibilities.

At one level there is nothing much we religious can do. We are witnessing one of the great paradoxes of universal life: rebirth through death. It is important, however, that we grieve our loss, experience our pain, stand still before our powerlessness, and pray for the grace to be open and receptive to the new, which will be ours to receive from God's creative abundance in God's own time. It is in this receptive ambience that we need to remember that we are co-creators with our creative God and that the new possibilities

13

being offered to us will be ours to receive and incarnate in appropriate structures. It is in this context of *receiving* and *incarnating* that the reflections of this book – on reframing – become eminently important.

Refounding is the work of divine initiative. *We* do not refound our orders and congregations; *God* does. In the refounding process, however, we are not passive onlookers but co-creative agents. God offers the gift; our privilege and co-responsibility is to respond in our capacity as human cultural beings. Influenced by our cultural milieu, we always incarnate our received wisdom in *structures* offered by our world. Which structures we choose or which ones we choose to try out, can often have life and death implications for the vision we are seeking to incarnate.

Mark's Gospel provides a timely reminder for us: 'For new wine you need fresh skins' (Mk 2:22). The human temptation is to couch our dreams and realities – old and new – in familiar 'wine-skins'; but that can spell disaster. The newness can be lost irretrievably. The graced moment has been reduced to human pragmatism; our will, rather than God's design, has jeopardised an otherwise hope-filled horizon.

The appropriate framework (wineskin) is not easily or readily discerned. Dialogue, reflection and prayer are essential prerequisites; but the wisdom and experience of ages past, along with the cultural stirrings of our time all provide important reference points. The tradition itself – in this case the deep story of the vowed life – can be a rich resource of wisdom and inspiration as we seek to discern appropriate options.

This book is an attempt to discover and expose some key frames of reference which hopefully will enlighten us through the confused maze of our contemporary experience. It attempts to name elements of our experience now resurfacing after not just centuries but millennia of suppression. By mining our deep historical story – to depths which relatively few writers have probed – we glimpse a panoramic view of religious life which offers a refreshing and challenging vision for the future. Our trajectory takes us far beyond the normative structures we take so much for granted into the exploration of the *values* and *aspirations* that bring the vowed life into being in the first place and nurture its growth and development in every age and culture known to humankind. It is this extended horizon, which stretches the human spirit and imagination to new limits, that underpins the suggested reframing we offer in this book.

Reframing is intended to be a liberating experience; undoubtedly it can also be a scary exercise. None of us likes abandoning the familiar, especially when it is validated by the weight of time and tradition. But in times of great cultural and historical change our options are quite limited: progress, regress, or stagnate. As a Christian people we are invited to espouse and promote 'the fullness of life' (Jn 10:10). Now, more than ever we are challenged anew – on behalf of God's people – to say *Yes* to life and to the largely disowned cultural and spiritual dimensions of the vowed life as a *value-radiation* experience. It is this new enlarged horizon that will engage us in the reflections and deliberations that follow.

CHAPTER ONE

The historical frame:
Reappropriating our universal story

Degenerate cultures may be content with fragmentary concepts that lack deeper meaning but vibrant cultures seek the contours of the whole of the reality they experience.

Erwin Laszlo

History is a process of unfolding patterns, not a series of punctuated or isolated events. History is a form of story populated by peoples, events and movements, but disclosing its deeper meaning in the narrative flow. History concerns an ongoing process, not a one-off product emanating from a battle, a truce or the infamous deeds of heroic people.

All history is sacred history. Every historical story captivates a will to meaning, often confused with a will to power. Historical processes are based on aspirations to engage with reality, rather than attempts which overtly seek to conquer and control it. The conscious overt actions, often extensively and crudely documented, can miss the richness, diversity and complexity of the subconscious will to meaning.

Religious life is only one of several movements that needs to be rescued from historical minimalism. Standard texts are dotted with ascetical feats of numerous outstanding men and a *few* outstanding women. The context tends to be exclusively ecclesiastical, rarely highlighting the prodigious cultural contributions of monastic and religious groups. And the geographical focus is largely Eurocentric, relegating the rest of the planet to coincidental anecdotes of relative (un)importance. Finally, there is the Christian model of the vowed life itself, often portrayed as totally unique, with nothing to contribute to or learn from the rich reservoir of religious life experience in the other great religions of the earth.

The Bedrock tradition of Egypt

The Christian model, in its popular form, is depicted as originating in Egypt around 250 CE when St Anthony pioneered the eremitical movement of courageous men and women, abandoning home and all they held dear for the austere life of penance and prayer in the mountainous desert region of northern Egypt. The devotee often lived alone, fasted for long hours and developed a heroic capacity to survive against the inner threat of insanity and the outer threat of alien forces.

Underpinning this ascetical ideal is the dominant metaphor of the *hero,* an image that has prevailed in Christian historiography until very recent times. The more heroic one tried to be, the more Godlike one became, and as one grew into the divine likeness, one transcended all earthly and bodily need, and eventually became transported into the divine realm itself. Consequently, the call to the monastic life came to be known as 'white martyrdom' (Malone 1950; Frend 1965), sacrificing all for the sake of Christ.

What motivated this apparently irrational drive? Historians offer a number of explanations, ranging from the deep fascination with the divine, which underpins all mystical movements to the more mundane reaction to the Church becoming more conformed to the world (via the privileges granted in the Edict of Constantine, 310 CE) and therefore abandoning the holiness and heroism of the martyrs. The fact that the early monastic movement emerged as an alternative to mainstream Christianity is a dimension of the religious life story that recurs many times in history and is rarely acknowledged for its deeper prophetic significance.

St Athanasius, in his biography of St Anthony, depicts

these first religious men (and women) as seekers of solitude. There seems to have been little room for a communal
dimension. But the writings of St Anthony himself (see
Chitty 1975) convey a different impression. The solitary
state was rarely lifelong and its prevailing structure tended
to be that of the *lavra* (Chitty 1966 p. 15), with three or
more people living in close proximity. Furthermore, as the
letters of St Anthony illustrate, people in their thousands
flocked to visit the desert monks, seeking their advice and
often attending to their temporal needs. Consequently to
suggest, as many historians do that the communal model is
largely unknown prior to the Pachomian developments in
Upper Egypt around 300 CE, is inaccurate and misleading.
What Pachomius achieved was the formalising of a ferment that had already come through many stages of growth
and development.

I do not wish to suggest that the account of Egyptian
monasticism is merely anecdotal or superficial. It is part of
a powerful story, and every good story thrives on over-
statement. But we must not turn a story into factual prose;
in that way we subvert its true meaning. The story of St
Anthony, and the movement it inspired is a counter-cultural witness to a culture ravaged in its craving for power,
and to a Church that had so conformed to the superficial
values of the time that it could no longer embody the
radical challenges of the new reign of God (Kingdom). Not
everything in the counter-culture is necessarily authentic
(e.g. the misguided myth of the imminent end of the world);
in every counter-culture light and shadow intermingle. In
this regard, the important contribution of Pachomius – as
noted by many scholars – was the purification of practices
that were in danger of becoming deviant (especially in the
realm of ascetical excesses).

John Cassian emerged as one of the first scholars of
Egyptian monasticism, claiming direct experience of the
Pachomian model (although that is doubtful), but declaring
his primary allegiance to the individualistic heroism of the
hermit. He had an impressive influence on the West, largely

inspiring the emergence of the wandering monk, the dominant monastic presence in the West until the founding of the Benedictines around 500 CE.

The Syrian tradition

For many years monastic scholars have debated whether religious life originated as a communal or an eremitical movement. This is not just an academic exercise of the selected few, but an issue of historical and theological import. Historically, it challenges us to explore pre-Egyptian forms such as the Covenantal groups of first- and second-century Syria, the community of the beloved disciple in John's Gospel, and pre-Christian groups such as the Essenes and the Therapeutae. Historically and theologically, we have given scant attention to the fact that many of the great founders and foundresses were accompanied by a small group of significant others in bringing their respective orders and congregations into being, the single best known example being that of St Ignatius and the seven companions.

I wish to submit that without the discernment and support of such a small group, many orders and congregations would never have come into being. Beyond the popular motif of historiography to focus on individual heroic achievements is a deeper communal wisdom, often underestimated and overlooked. At the heart of the (re)founding experience is the co-creativity of a *community* rather than an outstanding *individual*. Hence the need to retrieve a more coherent sense of the communal origins of the vowed life in Christianity, as well as the communal foundation of individual orders and congregations.

For this reason the developments of early Syria are particularly relevant (cf. Gribomont 1965; Nedungatt 1973; Murray 1974). Seeking to deepen their baptismal commitment, small groups convened, adopting a celibate way of life, sharing their goods and personal resources. Some con-

20

tinued to live in their own homes, others in shared households. Historical accounts suggest strong links with local churches in which they were considered a Christian elite. Charitable service to the community seems to have been an important aspect of their lives. Their eventual demise and the dispersion of their members into a more solitary existence is clearly the result of religious persecution and not, as is sometimes alleged a deepening of the spiritual life, leading to the more perfect solitary state. Their revival by Basil of Caesarea (*c.* 330-379 CE) is what gives Cappadocian monasticism its strong communitarian flavour, in contradistinction from the more solitary and heroic Egyptian model (see Gribomont 1965; Fedwick 1979).

Brown (1979) is among the few biblical scholars who highlight two dominant modes of discipleship in John's Gospel. There is the more structured and organised mode of following Jesus with Peter as its central figure. However, another group, for which John the beloved disciple is the focal person, pursues a more 'contemplative' loosely structured form of discipleship, favoured by Jesus, it would seem, as complementary aspect to the more structured mode. Have we here a possible biblical prototype of the vowed life?

In the Judaic tradition there is little concrete evidence for a form of monastic living although Desprez (1990) invites us to consider the Old Testament prophets, the Nazirites (Amos 2:11-12) and the Rechabites (who existed at the time of Jeremiah) as possible prototypes. Nonetheless, one has to ask whence did groups like the Essenes and the Therapeutae draw their inspiration? To what tradition do they belong? What was their role and function in the culture of the time? These are questions for which we seem to have few answers at the present time.

The great eastern tradition

It is quite possible that the few cases of Judaic monastic life known to us were inspired and influenced by develop-

21

ments in the Far East. Buddhist monasticism mediated through the *Shanga* (community), can be traced back to 500 BCE, and within a few hundred years had spread as far afield as Sri Lanka, Thailand, Japan and Tibet. The Hindu tradition largely confined to India, predates Christianity by over 2,000 years. A well known ancient trade route between Palestine and what we now know as the Indian subcontinent – following the route of the Tigris and Euphrates rivers – existed in early Christian times, facilitating a cross-fertilisation of ideas; a fact that is often noted but rarely explored in depth (to the best of my knowledge).

The Buddhist and Hindu expressions carry remarkable similarities – and problems – to Western Christian forms (see Henry and Swearer 1989; O'Murchu 1991). The underlying values are clearly identical. Customs and practices while adjusted to local environments exhibit numerous common strands. At one level, the Eastern forms (especially in Hinduism) seem more institutionalized. On the other hand, the cultural significance of the vowed life (what in subsequent chapters we call *liminality*) emerges in sharper and clearer relief in the Theravada Buddhist tradition than elsewhere.

Whether or not we can trace interdependent influence while interesting in itself, is not of immediate concern. What is more important is the tendency of the vowed life to surface in diverse faiths and cultures at different times in history. Consequently we also need to connect with the Tariqahs, the monastic system adopted by the Islamic faith (via Sufism), emerging initially in the eighth century and peaking between 1100 and 1300 CE (cf. Trimingham 1971). Today the Tariqahs continue to flourish in North Africa, Central Asia, Turkey, Arabia and Pakistan.

Also deserving of mention is the little known monastic movement within Sikhism of which the Udasi, the Nanaksar and the more loosely affiliated Nihang Singhs are among the better known groups. Contemporary Jewish developments such as the Kibbutzim and the Yeshiva seem to serve a purpose akin to that of monastic inculturation as do

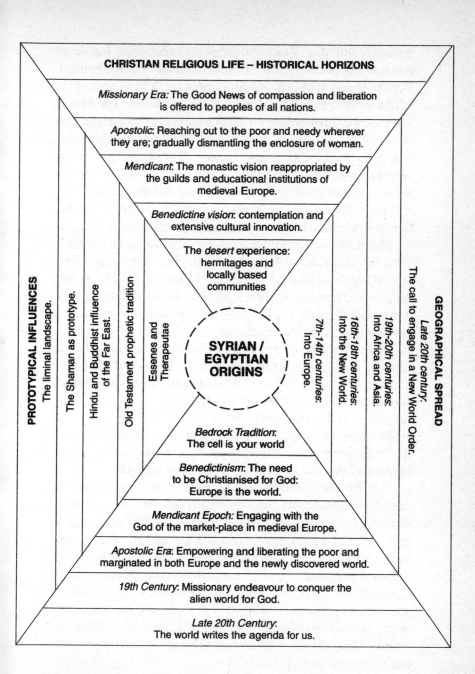

CHRISTIAN RELIGIOUS LIFE – HISTORICAL HORIZONS

Missionary Era: The Good News of compassion and liberation is offered to peoples of all nations.

Apostolic: Reaching out to the poor and needy wherever they are; gradually dismantling the enclosure of woman.

Mendicant: The monastic vision reappropriated by the guilds and educational institutions of medieval Europe.

Benedictine vision: contemplation and extensive cultural innovation.

The *desert* experience: hermitages and locally based communities

PROTOTYPICAL INFLUENCES

The liminal landscape.

The Shaman as prototype.

Hindu and Buddhist influence of the Far East.

Old Testament prophetic tradition

Essenes and Therapeutae

SYRIAN / EGYPTIAN ORIGINS

7th-14th centuries: Into Europe.

16th-18th centuries: Into the New World.

19th-20th centuries: Into Africa and Asia.

GEOGRAPHICAL SPREAD

Late 20th century: The call to engage in a New World Order.

Bedrock Tradition: The cell is your world

Benedictinism: The need to be Christianised for God: Europe is the world.

Mendicant Epoch: Engaging with the God of the market-place in medieval Europe.

Apostolic Era: Empowering and liberating the poor and marginated in both Europe and the newly discovered world.

19th Century: Missionary endeavour to conquer the alien world for God.

Late 20th Century: The world writes the agenda for us.

the many intentional communities (whether sacred or secular) that surface from time to time in all human cultures (cf. Barker 1982; Beckford 1986; Wittberg 1991).

As a historical story religious life manifests a range of forms and expressions across time and culture. Some of the better known modes are outlined in the diagram on page 23. The diagram depicts a vast range of historical forms, none of which may be considered superior to the others. History throws up its own expressions, as time and culture dictates. In fact, it seems to be the needs that are being addressed that provide the structural context through which we meet those needs, and these then become the normative structures for incarnating the vowed life. Contrary to the sanctioned tradition of fleeing the world and its earthly values religious life seems to thrive when it engages closely with the world of its time and with the urgent needs awaiting a courageously creative response.

From a historical viewpoint we cannot canonise any one form as being superior to all others. All have their place and their purpose. Nor may we exclude future expressions that are without precedent from the past e.g. a form of religious life for married people. The Spirit breathes where s(he) wills. The plurality of charismatic expression is unlikely to diminish; if anything, it will become more amorphous and diverse as history and culture unfolds.

Despite our inability to delineate with clear relief the dominant features of the vowed life universally, there is, nonetheless, something deeply pervasive and enduring in this global phenomenon. It is at the global level rather than in the particularity of each religious tradition and less so at the level of each order or congregation, that we are likely to discover the innate wisdom that makes this phenomenon special and culturally unique. As with contemporary science, the clue to ultimate meaning may no longer be in the 'basic building blocks', but in the wholistic interaction that comprises the greater totality.

The cyclic dimension

In the Christian tradition our approach to the history of religious life tends to be insular and ideological. Each religious family – e.g. Jesuit, Dominican, Franciscan, Ursuline etc. – tends to give its individual story priority over the more inclusive narrative of the larger reality to which each individual group belongs. We fail to realise that religious life itself is a gift to the world, and that each of our orders or congregations is a particular manifestation of this life, frequently with a specific purpose of relatively short duration. When this wider context is not duly acknowledged, individual groups perpetuate customs and mores that belong to another time and culture – ones that often hinder a more creative response to the contemporary world (e.g. wearing a form of religious garb that properly belongs to the Middle Ages). One also encounters strange rivalries (e.g. between the Jesuits and the Dominicans on philosophical or theological issues) that smack of a type of arrogance that seems alien to the Christian gospel and belongs more to a culture of competition, than one yearning for a more co-operative mode of attitude and behaviour.

The renewal of religious life as advocated by the Second Vatican Council sought to revive the individual uniqueness of each congregational charism. This guideline arose from deliberations that were quite poorly informed historically and theologically. While enabling some movement and new life to emerge, the guidelines of *Perfectae Caritatis* are inadequate to address the more complex issues facing religious life today. Contrary to what the Council Fathers may have intended, many orders and congregations have become narrowly focused on what they consider to be unique to themselves, although in fact several other groups hold almost identical value-systems. In some cases, therefore, the charism has become something of an ideology with some groups devoting much time, energy and questionable amounts of money to the maintenance and development of centres and resources focused in an exclusive, ideological way on the founding person. As Lee (1989) points out, charism was never intended to be a fixed feast, and to make it so tends to compound our confusion rather than clarify our vision.

Our explicit focus on individual charisms tends to emulate the popular rendition of the religious life story as a series of disjointed facts and anecdotal happenings. Religious life as *movement* through the ebb and flow of particular historical cycles has been given scant attention. This more wholistic view of our history is very much a development of the present century, with the French Jesuit Raymond Hostie (1972) as its main proponent.

The cyclic thesis presents such a simplified picture that it immediately generates unease and suspicion. Surely it can't be that simple! It suggests that religious life in the Christian tradition evolves in cycles of approximately 300 years, each cycle manifesting a series of developmental stages, characterised by growth and expansion reaching a climax, and then progressively declining towards a critical stage, culminating in the extinction of several groups or the revitalisation of others in the context of a new cycle. In the Christian story thus far, six cycles have been identified:

The foundational phase:	250 – 600 CE
The first Benedictine era:	600 – 900 CE
The second Benedictine era:	900 – 1200 CE
The Mendicant cycle:	1200 – 1500 CE
Era of the Apostolic Religious:	1500 – 1800 CE
The Missionary epoch:	1800 – ?

According to Hostie an estimated 75% of all orders and congregations have become extinct; of the 104 male institutions founded up to 1500 CE, only 25 are still in existence. However, we also note that several groups (including the Benedictines Franciscans, Dominicans, Jesuits, Ursulines) have revitalised with the onset of one or more new cycles. We need to emphasise that the new lease of life for older groups is the result of adopting the new vision of each fresh cycle, rather than reviving and maintaining a previous tradition. A charism continues to be fruitful when it is capable of inspiring a meaningful response to the urgent needs of each new epoch, rather than adherence to the traditions and mores of a previous era.

Historians in general dislike the cyclic approach because it lacks rigorous historical analysis, and its findings are open to lateral, rather than linear, interpretation. In each cycle there is a clear developmental progression of expanding numbers, apostolic impact and cultural influence, followed by an equally long phase of decline and ultimate crisis. At several stages the 'why' is unclear. For example, the rise of the Franciscans at the beginning of the thirteenth century was characterised by extensive inner strife on the understanding of poverty, and by 1300 CE the Franciscan family was already divided into several splinter groups. Despite all this the Franciscans proved to be an outstanding force for ecclesial and cultural renewal throughout that entire time. Another example: around 1750 CE it is estimated that there were 400,000 religious in the world (mainly in Europe) and apparently there was nothing to suggest an imminent crisis. Fifty years later, in the wake of the French Revolution, there were less than 50,000 – a reduction of almost 90%. Is it by accident that this decline coincides with the end of a 300 year cycle?

It seems to me that the cyclic approach cannot be understood purely in rational nor solely in historical terms. Other factors – sociological, psychological and spiritual – come into play. In fact, we are dealing with a multi-disciplinary frame of reference (as employed by Cada and Alia 1979), rather than one based on any one field of learning – which is what makes the cyclic approach especially commendable. Central to this framework is the Christian paradigm of death and resurrection or the Eastern construct of birth-death-rebirth.

Each cycle commences with a world in turmoil evoking from creative visionaries (like Benedict, Bernard, Francis,

Angela Merici and Mary Ward) a response to the acute needs of the time, and the birthing of a movement inspired to bring fresh light and hope to the waiting world. Political and social unrest, along with spiritual atrophy and moral decadence, characterise the world scene into which orders and congregations tend to be born. And these groups tend to be at the cutting edge of fresh initiatives as they inculturate the *chaos* with a sense of dynamism and fresh creativity.[1]

While the groups keep their focus on the world and its needs their efforts are blessed with growth and progress. When the focus shifts from the world to the group's own power, success and survival – what Cada and Alia (1979) call the point of utopian flaw – the group loses its bearings. The ideal they now serve is no longer God at the heart of the world, but an idol fashioned to their own image and likeness. This is the beginning of the downward slant, as predictable and irreversible as the proverbial slide on the sharp face of a cliff.

This is one of the most baffling and mysterious dimensions of the cyclic approach: the inevitable decline once the group abdicates its primary focus on the world. A classic attempt to reverse this process is the rise of the Cistercians in the late eleventh century, whose task was to halt the Benedictine morass and recapture a way of life true to the original vision of St Benedict. For some 50 years they enjoyed growth and expansion. They reclaimed the contemplative *raison d'etre* and instituted the lay brotherhood so that the monks would not become immersed in the commercialism of the world. And they located their monasteries in marshy lands, so that they would not be distracted by the allurements of the business world. By the end of the eleventh century, the marshes were converted into lucrative agricultural terrains (thanks largely to the lay brothers) and the Cistercians were now as 'corrupt' as those they sought to rescue. The way forward for religious life was not a revitalisation of Benedictinism, but a quality of response that would encounter and engage with the emerging world of the high Middle Ages. It took visionar-

28

ies like Francis and Dominic to make the daring and appropriate response.

Consequently, the cycle, in its downward slant seems to have no option other than to go right down into the Calvary experience of diminishment, chaos and death, out of which will spring the shoots of new life. Perhaps the main reason why so few groups succeed in revitalising is because so many are reluctant to face death. It is much easier (although painfully difficult) to live in a state of denial. In that state our eyes and ears (and hearts) are closed – to God and to the world. Our own survival is our subconscious (sometimes conscious) preoccupation; ironically, it is the very thing that ensures our ultimate extinction.

From these cursory reflections it may be apparent that the cycles referred to above have historical significance not merely for religious life but for the wider Church and world as well. All seemed well in European religious life in 1750 CE with many of the 400,000 religious proclaiming the Gospel and witnessing to it in a vast range of charitable and educational projects. But the spiritual focus was distinctly Jansenistic, preoccupied with the salvation of the *soul* in order to gain admittance to *another* world (heaven) and thus escape from this world. The global vision of the new reign of God (Kingdom), with its focus on the world and the creation of right relationships, marked by justice, love, peace and liberation had been largely, if not totally, betrayed, not merely by religious, but by the Church itself. The prevailing spirituality had become disembodied, incestuous and anti-incarnational. The French Revolution served as an external catalyst for a crisis that was already imminent. The diminution of religious life towards the end of the apostolic era was brought about by *internal* malaise rather than by *external* opposition.

The rise and fall of religious groups within the various cycles highlights the factors that augment growth and decline in the vowed life. Decline is instigated primarily by lack of focus, or, in more modern terms, a diminution in the sense of mission. Instead of listening attentively to the world and its needs, religious become enmeshed in trying to protect their own identity, survival and internal needs. As the focus shifts inwards it is not uncommon to find wealth accumulating, material goods and possessions accreting, self-aggrandisement consuming time and energy, while the sense of prayer and contemplation deteriorates and sometimes disappears. Internal squabbles and conflicts may abound but are rarely addressed, as in the case of a dysfunctional family where the discomfort of delusion is more tolerable than the pain of truth and honesty. As the malaise deepens, inertia increases; even people in leadership can find themselves totally incapacitated. The power of the dysfunctional system undermines the will to live in many of its constituent parts.

These features of the declining phase occur frequently in the history of religious life as the various cycles move into contraction. Some of those features (e.g. the accumulation of wealth, deterioration in prayer life, and dysfunctional relationships) reoccur throughout the course of so many different cycles that it is baffling and deeply disturbing that we can be so blind to the lessons of history. Cycle in, cycle out, we repeat the same mistakes over and over again!

What are equally clear are the dynamics that make for growth and fresh life. The primary factor is the unambiguous and unencumbered response to the urgent needs of the emerging world. Allegiance to the Church, although often highlighted in historical documents, is not of central importance. The *world*, rather than the *Church*, is the primary focus of every fresh development in the unfolding story of Christian religious life.

The inner freedom to listen deeply and the outer initiative to respond in new and fresh ways are the key variables. Hence the need for already established groups to die and let go of their previous vision and ideals. The great founders and foundresses read the signs of the times in a provocatively challenging and disturbing way. Respect for tradition, building on the past, and ensuring continuity are issues

30

that did not much concern them. Their focus was on the *future* – the creation of something radically new to address the fresh needs.

It is this focus on the world, rather than on the *Church*, that makes the history of religious life unique. There is a distinctive global ambience to every foundation in our history. Even the several French groups which emerged during the nineteenth century, while founded to address very specific local needs, largely aligned themselves with the Church's missionary outreach within the first 20 years of their existence and adopted a global focus for their life and mission. Even the early Benedictines, set up in a distinctive communal structure thus declaring the wandering monk to be redundant, rapidly became a powerful missionary force and, despite their vow of stability, moved freely across what is now mainland Europe and the Soviet states. Innate to the religious life vocation is the call to serve the world in its full global embrace. It is precisely when we fail in this capacity that we Religious become a contradiction to ourselves and an anachronism to the surrounding culture.

Religious life, therefore, although firmly rooted in the religion and ecclesiology of Christianity, is a *cultural*, rather than a *religious*, phenomenon. The Christian historical story points out beyond itself in the direction of the world. Our role in that global context is what we will explore in the next two chapters.

CHAPTER TWO

The cultural frame:
Transcending religious categories

Once we have fabricated our identities we almost inevitably identify ourselves with the fabrications of the empire.

Mary Jo Leddy

In the Western world we tend to divide everything into sets of opposing pairs. Distinctions between good and evil, man and woman, God and man(kind), East and West, black and white are frequently employed. Useful though these distinctions are for daily discourse they emanate from a deeper level of consciousness, and therefore they can blind rather than enlighten, confuse rather than clarify, and diminish rather than enlarge our perceptions of reality.

At the subconscious level these distinctions take on a *dualistic* significance whereby we attribute deep-seated values to the opposing poles. Opposites are often pitched so far apart that there is no reconciling middle ground. The grey area in between where real life issues are frequently negotiated, is considered to be for the unenlightened, the confused and the uninformed. Everything must be either right or wrong, and the clearer we are about that, the better for everybody.

It begins to feel imperialistic, and so indeed it is. Christianity is particularly susceptible to this imperialistic mode because of its early links with Greek philosophy, which advocated the dualistic distinction in thought, word and deed. Everything had to have an opposite, against which it could be measured and evaluated. In this way the total reality, which needs both 'opposites' to be understood fully, frequently escaped attention.

In popular Christianity some of the outstanding dualisms include: earth v. heaven, grace v. nature, natural v. supernatural, body v. soul, sacred v. secular. Consequently, all that pertained to religion, church, God and spirituality was labelled *sacred*; all that affects life in the human earthly and global culture was labelled *secular,* and therefore deemed to be alien to God and to the things of the Spirit. Although many of these dualisms have little appeal today, they still exert immense influence on how we understand our various traditions, and this is particularly true in their application to the vowed life.

In the early 1970s when I began studying the history of religious life in Christianity, I informed my tutor that I was intrigued by similar developments in the other great religions, and I expressed a wish to extend my research to include these. Gently but firmly I was advised to steer clear of what were essentially 'pagan' developments, which were only pale reflections of our Christian inheritance and probably were inspired by Christianity in the first place. (I now realise how appallingly ignorant my tutor was.) It took almost ten years to venture beyond that restricted horizon, and explore for myself those vastly complex and fascinating processes that comprise the vowed life in its global context (see O'Murchu 1991 pp. 14-32).

The Shamanic prototype

And then I had to engage with some intriguing questions: whence did Hinduism (the oldest known of the religions) inherit this ideal and its accompanying institutionalization? Are there prototypes which predate the great religions themselves and if so can or need they be called *religious* in any formal sense of the word? Thus I encountered the strange and fascinating world of *shamanism* often depicted as a folk religion, but more popularly invoked today as an esoteric new-age mode of trance and enlightenment.

Shamanism is an ancient spiritual praxis, known to many prehistoric societies, dating back to at least 10,000 BCE. The shamanic vocation even when inherited through a family line is considered to be a special calling which sets the person apart for special service. In biblical terms the place of the shaman (and shamanness) is in the world but not of it. The shaman is a mediator between the people and the higher divine powers, and the mediating role is not just in praying or beseeching the divinity (as the *priest* is empowered to do); it is often effected in trance-like behaviour, in which the shaman seems to embody some of the divine powers themselves.

Shamanism is often associated with *healing* and in many ancient cultures the shaman and the medical practitioner were one and the same person. Shamanic healing, however, is distinctively wholistic in nature, calling forth not just renewed health but a challenge to change and improve behaviour and attitudes in significant ways. In this capacity the shaman is as much a spiritual guide as a source of practical help.

The shamanic vocation is quite ambiguous in nature, suspended between a very pragmatic integrated presence with the people and an exalted pseudo-divine role, a type of embodiment of people's deepest yearnings and aspirations. For example, when the ancient hunters wanted to kill animals to procure meat they often gathered the beasts at the verge of a cliff, then sent for the shaman, whose task it was to push them over (usually by frenzied trance-like behaviour). When the animals were dead, the meat was removed under the supervision of the shaman, who then took the bones for a special 'religious' burial.

In prehistoric societies the shaman and priest although perceived at times to be identical, do in fact serve distinctly different purposes. The priest plays a much more institutionalised role *within* the formal structures of society and seems to be more the product of formal religion, with the specific task of offering sacrifice to appease or implore the gods (see Eisler 1988 pp. 84-85). The shaman has a much more comprehensive, open-ended role and, although more close to the people at one level, does not belong to the 'ordinary' realm of reality. His spiritual versatility is in a very different league from, and deemed to be superior to, that of the priest.

Quite an extensive literature exists on shamanism much of which focuses on the esoteric and at times bizarre behaviour associated with shamanic trance and ecstasy. One is reminded of the parallel tendency in many 'Lives' of the saints to focus attention on outstanding ascetical achievements. This quality of hagiography runs a great risk of missing the essential message embodied in these special personages.

The literature refers only to individual shamans (as far as I can discover). There are no records of communities or groups of shamans although Eliade (1964) does refer to a shamanic fraternity (p. 316) and to an auxiliary group called 'sons of the shaman' (p. 117). But there is a very definite communitarian ambience: recognition as a shaman is bestowed only by the whole community (Eliade p. 17) and many aspiring shamans renounce the profession if the clan does not grant unanimous approval.

Eliade (p. 6) suggests that shamanism is better understood in a mystical, rather than in a religious, context. He notes the comparison with monks of the Christian tradition, but chooses not to develop this seminal insight. He describes shamans as the elect whose ecstatic experience gives them access to the sacred on behalf of the wider community; parallels with the Old Testament prophetic tradition are readily recognisable.

The Prophetic strand

Elijah, Jeremiah, Isaiah and Amos are among the outstanding prophetic figures of Old Testament times. Most contemporary writers on religious life consider these prophetic people to be prototypical for the vowed life of Christianity. In the Old Testament the prophet and king are juxtaposed, with the priest on the same side as the king. The king represents the royal power, which is perceived to be divinely instituted and therefore validates the human urge to structure and control. The maintenance and preservation of the *status quo* is central to the king's perception of his power and duty. The prophet serves as a perpetual reminder of the free and creative God under whom no set of human institutions can ever be finally and dogmatically validated. The prophetic movement, therefore, seeks to develop and nurture the non-institutionalised dimensions: the dreams, the hopes, the aspirations which the formal structures are intended to mediate, but which are often stifled and subverted when the institutions assume a self-perpetuating myth and become ends unto themselves. For prophetic ministry all human and political reality must be kept radically open to the new and surprising creativity of God at the heart of the world (Brueggemann 1978, 1986; Chittister 1994).

The task of the prophet is to be counter-cultural to highlight alternative values and ways of being, to keep open the larger view of reality, and to challenge those structures and systems which tend to stifle and stultify the divine-human co-creativity. The tendency of the formal system is to become a god unto itself; the task of the prophet is to challenge and denounce all partial or false idols, pointing continuously to the God who embraces all and whose reality can never be formalised or mediated in any one set of laws or institutions.

The prophetic vocation, therefore, is *cultural* rather than *religious*. The prophet seeks to safeguard and foster the spiritual and more wholistic values that underpin life in its fundamental meaning. The prophetic task is to be as inclusive as possible and contest all movements that veer towards exclusivity – which in religious terms often lead to idolatry, bigotry and sectarianism. The prophets, therefore, are not particularly enamoured of religion; their vision of God – and the divine plan for creation – far outstretches

36

what formalised religion embodies and seeks to convey (particularly in Jeremiah and Ezekiel).

Prophetic ministry as depicted in the Old Testament, could be described by three words: contemplative, political and inclusive. The prophets perceive in depth; they strive to see the whole picture as God sees it and they struggle to attend as fully as possible to the divine unfolding within the whole of creation. One is reminded of Joan Chittister's description of the contemplative task as '... the ability to see through and to see into and to see despite and to see without blindness. It is the ability to see a whole world rather than a partial one' (Chittister 1990 p. 52). We glean a similar vision from the writings of Thomas Merton:

> Contemplation is the keen awareness of the interdependence of all things. It is a sudden gift of awareness, an awakening to the real within all that is real. It is the response to a call from the God who has no voice and who speaks in everything that is and who most of all speaks to the depths of our own being words meant to answer God, to echo God, and even in some ways to contain and signify God (quoted in Chittister 1990 p. 51).

Since the political arena is the sphere in which values are inculturated in structures and institutions the prophet claims the right to have a say, not necessarily in the capacity of an officially elected representative, but as one missioned to be the voice of the voiceless and an ambassador for those deeper values that tend to be subverted by the political process. Amos dared to question the source and purpose of power and prosperity in Israel; he cited war crimes, tax foreclosures and failures at the gate, where elders met to mete out justice – but decidedly against the poor. Hosea confronted the temple priests for colluding with political powers promoting the practice of (royal) religion, rather than the righteousness which religion was supposed to promote and develop. Isaiah lived at a time of massive military power, which he vehemently denounced as he saw thousands of defenceless, vulnerable people slaughtered in the name of national honour. Micah came from a situation where he watched people being forced into labour camps to build projects for the benefit of the rich; he protested on behalf of the poor; he prophesied for truth, not for profit.

In all prophetic ministry there is what Heschel (1960) calls 'prophetic pathos'. Focusing on the prophetic vocation, biblical scholars devote undue attention to the divine origin of the call and not enough discernment on the prophetic praxis itself, with its distinctly political and social aspects (see Hobbs 1985). Retrieving the cutting edge of prophetic witness is an urgent issue of our times, a task that cannot be undertaken without some measure of political and socio-economic engagement.

Where and how to place one's political clout is a dauntingly difficult challenge for any person or movement striving to be genuinely prophetic in the world and Church of our time. The political system itself is largely corrupt, and becoming progressively dysfunctional (see Drucker 1989; Wilson Schaef 1987). While seeking to confront the mainstream political system and denounce its oppression of the weak and marginalised, prophetic visionaries must also dream alternative ways of political engagement, outside and beyond the formal structures. Socio-political networks such as Worldwatch, Friends of the Earth, Greenpeace and several feminist groups exert a much more distinctive shift in political consciousness than do most parliamentarians. Forming closer alliances with such groups may be a much more prophetic gesture than forging links with what in many parts of our world, is a corrupt regime that has largely outlived its usefulness.

And in the political denunciation and contestation one of the prophet's unique roles is that of safeguarding and promoting *inclusivity* as a fundamental cultural and spiritual value. Prophetic witness, therefore, will opt for and foster systems that cherish openness, fluidity and flexibility, organizations that strive to be more truly and justly at the service of people's real needs, and movements that seek to respect and integrate the human-divine co-creativity.

The prophet is very much a person among the people yet the rationale of the prophetic calling is complex and enormously difficult to discern. The vocational ambience is personal, interpersonal (communitarian) and planetary. The prophet knows what's going on – intuitively, rather than rationally or intellectually. In the prophetic imagination, reality is writ large. The whole picture is perceived, and the contradictions which others find irreconcilable are held in creative tension. Dualisms have no place in the prophetic imagination. It is the unity of all reality – the whole that is greater than the sum of the parts – that engages the prophet. At the heart of that engagement is a passion for *justice* (elucidated at length by Barr 1995), a burning desire to cherish and foster the diversity and richness of the total picture, with equality and hope for every singular dimension. It is not merely a people-centred justice but one that includes all creatures (and the planet) who tend to be excluded and oppressed by the prevailing dominant culture.

Prophets elicit admiration, but they also evoke antagonism. The prophet disturbs; and frequently this happens through apparently contradictory behaviour, rather than through preached word or inspirational action. To the mainstream culture the prophet is always an enigma, a maverick and usually a nuisance. Above all, the prophet poses a threat to the stability and security of the *status quo* and that threat will be removed rather than confronted; engaging with it involves too many risks of exposing vulnerability – even corruption – thus confirming the bitter truth that the prophet openly proclaims, and the institution desperately tries to deny. It is no easy task to follow in the prophetic way.

The Old Testament prophetic tradition consists of outstanding *individuals* (Jeremiah, Isaiah, Hosea, etc). In the New Testament apart from Jesus himself, only a few people are accredited with prophetic power, John the Baptist being the best known. So what has happened to the great tradition of the Old Testament? In responding to this question, biblical scholars claim that what the prophets of old pointed to has now come to fruition in the person and ministry of Jesus, and, consequently, prophets are not needed any more. This response scarcely does justice to the deeper meaning of the prophetic call, and instead I choose to follow the view which claims that in the New Testament the prophetic nucleus has shifted from *individuals* to *communities*.

It is in the context of community that the prophetic vocation is mediated in the New Testament. Some obvious examples include the gathering of the early Christians as outlined in Acts 2 and 4. It is also worth citing the perceptive insight of Boff (1986 pp. 51ff) who claims that the twelve apostles are significant not as twelve *individuals*, but as *the twelve*, representing communally the twelve tribes of Israel. In a similar vein we note that, on those occasions when Jesus is taking time apart to discern, he frequently takes with him the core group of Peter, James and John.

The suggestion that the New Testament prophetic focus has shifted from individuals to communities has significant implications for our emerging theology of religious life and for the reframing envisaged in the present work. It also invites a re-examination of our tendency to view the origins of religious life in the Christian tradition as primarily eremitical, rather than communitarian (see p. 20 above). But it evokes even more profound considerations relating to the *cultural* context of the vowed life and its inherent value orientation. Is there an older tradition, even predating shamanism, that embodies communitarian values of enduring importance? Can we now name – maybe for the first time – a still more ancient strand of the vowed life and the values it embodies on behalf of the wider culture? That we will attempt to do in the next Chapter when we explore the notion of *liminality*.

Value radiation centres

Meanwhile, we note the new horizons that are opening up for the vowed life in its cultural, as well as in its religious frame of reference (cf. diagram on p. 42). It is not entirely new to adopt the Old Testament prophetic movement as prototypical for religious life;[2] but for many readers the proposed links with shamanism and its long historical tradition (of at least 10,000 years) will be quite novel.

In creating these links I am not simply trying to establish that the history of the vowed life is much older than we had heretofore conceived. My main interest is in the symbolic spiritual import of these developments:

a. They have a unique capacity to provide intense value radiation for the wider culture.[3]
b. Their witness is fundamentally counter-cultural, indicating that human society at all times benefits from such challenge, although the dominant culture will strive to dampen and subvert its impact.

These two points are interrelated. Both touch on the human need for *values*, and the human orientation to attribute moral, aesthetic, political, economic, or social importance to some things and not to others. Contemporary western culture tends to underestimate values; what we often call a value-free society is effectively a *valueless* one, where everything from the dysfunctional kitchen toaster to the ill or handicapped person is likely to be discarded because they are no longer 'valuable'. We tend to value objects and people in terms of productivity and their ability to accrue wealth. This breeds a climate of functionalism and competitiveness, the deleterious effects of which are all too conspicuous in our dwindling capitalistic culture (see Fox 1994, esp. ch. 1).

The counter-culture to western capitalism is one that seeks to reclaim the spiritual and human worth of people,

THE CULTURAL FRAME

This diagram is a type of Mandala, with the dominant patriarchal prototype in centre place, and somewhat suspended in the background are the largely disowned cultural elements of the vowed life that we seek to reclaim today.

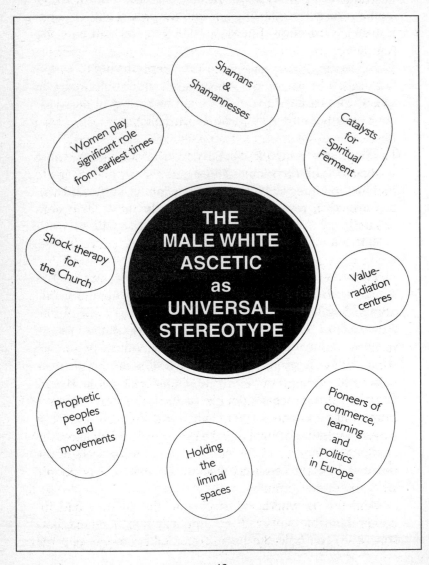

whether they are functionally productive or not. The sacredness of the human being in his/her God-given humanity is granted primary consideration. Unfortunately, this otherwise laudable aspiration, emerging in a predominantly dualistic culture, ensued in human worth being juxtaposed to planetary well-being, creating yet another destructive value system. Thus the counter-culture now swings towards ecological and environmental values, without which the entire human enterprise is in jeopardy. We humans cannot hope to live in dignity and integrity without fostering the dignity and integrity of creation itself. We are one with the planet we inhabit and with the cosmos to which we belong.

A genuine counter-culture is always characterised by a desire to realign disparate fragmented or alienated parts.[4] A larger picture is invoked, and what the dominant culture wishes to exclude or cut off, the counter-culture strives to include and integrate. Long-lost wisdom or subverted values are often revoked – subconsciously rather than consciously.

It is at the subconscious level that counter-cultures thrive, reawakening primordial values and long-lost ideals. This process known to social scientists as *recapitulation*, digs deep into the collective unconscious retrieving past wisdom and energy, to enhance and create a forward leap into new ways of being. An example explored at greater length in chapter four, is that of the rise of modern feminism, which draws a great deal of inspiration from the goddess culture of pre-patriarchal times, dating back some 40,000 years. In this process of rediscovering the past we have little conscious control over what will emanate. We can expect a mixture of light and darkness, order and chaos, the challenge of unity and the fear of disintegration. Fear of the power of the unconscious shadow is what makes people wary of counter-cultures.

And this is where we touch into the abstract and incomprehensible power of the prophetic and shamanic person: s(he) can hold the paradoxes, and even entertain the

43

contradictions, without being demolished by them. Prophetic people do not fit comfortably into the mainstream culture, because they embody a more complex and diffuse consciousness, whereby they are often unsure and unclear in their own minds, frequently suspended between the worlds of conscious reality and subconscious possibility. This is the liminal space, dauntingly difficult to enculturate in terms of 'ordinary daily life', as we shall highlight in the next chapter.

Meanwhile, we need to expose our beings to the prophetic experience, especially the challenge to transcend our man-made dualisms which neatly divide and segregate but alienate us from the wholism and universalism without which we cannot hope to find our true human and planetary identity. It is the 'untidiness' and open-endedness of this process that scares us, and deprives us of the insight and wisdom with which we could more readily comprehend our true role as children of Mother Earth.

We have described counter-cultures as intense value-radiation centres, experiences wherein key values are intensified and people are challenged to engage with those values in their own daily lives. The focus is usually on values that are under threat, or whose importance has been thwarted by subversive or oppressive forces.

A great deal of contemporary counter-culture unfolds around the decline of patriarchy and its accompanying values of domination, manipulation, control, rationalism and linear logic.[5] We take those values so much for granted that many fail to see a problem with them. Nor do many people realise that they have dominated our world for some 10,000 years, pioneering a culture of anthropomorphism, with human beings assuming idolatrous interference, with deleterious consequences for people and planet alike.

The emerging counter-culture focuses strongly on reclaiming and restoring the power of the feminine not merely for balance, but to complete the co-creative interaction which requires both dimensions in continuous mutuality. This attempt at redressing the balance is beginning to impinge upon every field of contemporary culture, most notably in ecology, feminism, sexuality and spirituality.

Value-radiation, therefore, may refer to the intensification of certain values, or alternatively to the task of restoring the complementarity of value-polarity when this has been interfered with by one-sided emphasis. In either case, the aspiration arises subconsciously within those cultures which have been impoverished and deprived of that fullness of life to which all living beings aspire.

These considerations invite contemporary religious women and men to examine afresh the purpose of their existence, and face urgent questions regarding their role in the world today. Have we allowed the vowed life to become so narrow and functional that it is in danger of usurping its divine mandate to be a catalyst for mediating and radiating deep values? Have we betrayed our ancient roots in shamanic witness and in prophetic contestation? Have we allowed ourselves to be conformed to ecclesiastical and political systems whose energy is invested in maintaining the *status quo*, rather than in counter-cultural activity?

In a word, is our cultural frame of reference so narrow and restrictive – couched in minimalism, legalism, extrinsicism and juridicism (Merkle 1992, p. 82) – that it is stultifying what is uniquely ours as a prophetic liminal movement? This may well be the most urgent question confronting religious life today. Hopefully, the reflections of the present chapter will help to refocus our questions and concerns, and encourage us to reclaim something of that great tradition which belongs to the vowed life in its deeper cultural frame of reference.

CHAPTER THREE

The cultural frame:
The liminal context

If religious life, by its very structure, involves a certain abnormality, then that life will experience crisis when it seeks to become normal and when it is no longer lived in the desert or on the frontier

Jon Sobrino

In suggesting that religious life can be traced back to prehistoric times, our primary concern is not with the vowed life in its *institutional* mode, but rather with its underlying *value system*. Shamanism and Old Testament prophecy tend to be described as major cultural movements of historical or religious import. Often studies of them focus on the *facts* that comprise the story. My concern is the story itself, and especially the *values* it embodies and mediates.

In the contemporary western world, *values* are often taken for granted. We speak of value-free science or value-free judgements, in which we attempt an evaluation that will not bias or prejudice the outcome. What, in effect, we mean is *value-less*, and not *value-free*. As relativity and quantum theory (in physics) illustrate so well, the observer is always inherent to the process of observation; there is no such thing as a totally objective perception or point of view. A value-free evaluation is impossible; a value-less judgement is one that is *biased against values*.

Values smack of religious overtones, and in our western dualistic culture we strive to keep the sacred and the secular as far apart as possible. But, as is often the case, the rigid simplicity of dualistic categories confuses, rather than clarifies, the essential issue. We consider sacred and religious to be synonymous, and we assume that secularity has nothing to do with either. What a naive set of assumptions but also what a confusing and potentially destructive one!

Many people in today's world are rightly suspicious of religion; it breeds sectarianism, bigotry, arrogance and a great deal of warfare. Many people abandon religion, but continue to live morally responsible and spiritual lives. One of the most urgent issues of our time is to differentiate clearly between *religion* and *spirituality*.

Religion, in many parts of the world, is in deep crisis; spirituality enjoys a significant revival taking place outside, rather than within, our religious institutions. It is often in the absence of religion that people rediscover their spiritual core, that inner space that relentlessly seeks meaning and purpose in oneself, in others and in the universe. We are all endowed with this innate capacity which often remains dormant and underdeveloped, possibly for an entire lifetime. For some it is the salient well-spring that nourishes their vitality, hope and joy providing an inner sense of contentment, a capacity to serve others generously and kindly, and an openness to the mystery and goodness of life (without, necessarily, an explicit faith in God). For others the spiritual orientation, repressed and often frustrated, is projected outwards in excessive devotion to power, possessions, or pleasure. In all cases, we are worshipping a 'God' because our very nature moves in that direction.

Spirituality and value radiation

Zappone (1991) describes spirituality as the relational component of lived experience. I reflect on my experience and strive to listen to its 'message'. I discern the meaning of the message(s) by focusing on its various relational aspects, because my capacity to relate and my desire to do so is that realm of experience in which I am most closely related to God; it is the core of my spiritual self. At this spiritual centre, everything takes on *value* of a positive life-

47

giving nature, or of an alienating or destructive vein. The values may not be clear-cut; in fact they rarely are. Negotiating and understanding the grey area(s) comprises the perpetual struggle of humans from time immemorial.

There are fundamental values to which all humans aspire. These include: truth, honesty, integrity, love, goodness, the union of opposites. They may be called *archetypal:* basic values to which people of every race and culture aspire. How these values are transmitted, mediated and enculturated will vary immensely from one time to another throughout the various cultures and epochs of history.

The conviction that key values are universally shared is highly disputed among theorists of the various sciences. Some claim that all values are learned; others that they are culturally transmitted; others still claim that they are mediated on an universal scale through something akin to the Jungian notion of the *collective unconscious*. According to the Jungian view our universe is endowed with a conscious energy (what contemporary physicists call *the creative vacuum*), a well-spring of possibility from which emanate the deep dreams, hopes and aspirations which we all inherit. Although divinely endowed (according to Jung), what is mediated to us through the collective unconscious consists of both light and darkness (the shadow). We cannot change what we inherit, but since we ourselves contribute to this 'pooled wisdom', we can change the future nature and impact of the collective unconscious.

In Jungian terms the content of the collective unconscious is mediated through archetypes, symbols and rituals, many, but not all, of which are religious in nature. In Jung's own words:

> There are many symbols that are not individual but collective in their nature and origin. These are chiefly religious images; their origin is so far buried in the mystery of the past that they seem to have no human source. But they are in fact collective representations, emanating from primeval dreams and creative fantasies.

As such, these images are involuntary, spontaneous manifestations, and by no means intentional inventions.

(Jung 1968 pp. 41-42)

Many of the recurring themes in the great religions belong to the realm of universal archetypal values as Bausch (1975 pp. 70-71) indicates:

That is why certain basic myths called *archetypal* keep popping up. Some are the sharing of food... denoting the sharing of the very substance that keeps one alive; hence the supreme hospitality, brotherhood, fellowship; the shedding of blood as a loss of vitality, and drinking it as drinking the source of life. There are Gods who died and rose again to explain the seasons. Miracles were used as proof of divine power. Virgin births were spoken of. The point is that these symbols are not unique to Christianity nor should they be. They are basic myths that explain humanity's eternal hopes, answers to the meaning of life, birth, death, tragedy and suffering.

Many ceremonies which today we would describe as religious originally evolved as *rites of passage* rituals, used to mark and celebrate important moments of transition in human or planetary life (e.g. birth, puberty, menopause, death, the first rainfall, the food season, the hunt, etc.). It was while studying the significance of rites of passage that the Dutch anthropologist Arnold Van Gennep coined the term *liminality* (in 1908), which will occupy our considerations for the remainder of this chapter.

Thus far we have referred to *values*, which we claim have universal impact, exemplified in the shared spiritual (but not necessarily religious) inheritance of people and planet alike, and mediated through various rites and symbols. Liminality seems to be one of the most pervasive and profound forms of value-radiation that we humans have adopted, and becomes a key focus for reframing the vowed life in the world of our time.

The nature of liminality

The concept is derived from the Latin word *limen* meaning threshold and refers to those ritualisations which focus on marginality, or the experience of being at a frontier. The trend in many cultures, past and present, to stand apart from direct engagement with the world – whether it be the daily option to rest, relax and recreate; the spiritual desire to reflect pray or meditate; the annual family holiday; or the experience of going on a retreat – illustrates the pervasive and universal nature of liminality. But this is merely the *conscious* expression – the things we choose to do or feel urged to do, to 'balance' the pressures of life, or to 'escape' from the humdrum of daily experience.

The real nature of liminality is discernible at the deeper subconscious realm where the yearnings and aspirations of the heart seek mediation and expression. Liminality is a subconscious drive for wholeness, for completeness, for tangible connection with the Originating Mystery which impinges upon our lives, whether we consciously acknowledge it or not. It is an inner orientation of the human spirit, that defies logical or rational explanation.

Van Gennep's seminal insights remained largely unexplored until the 1950s, when the anthropologists Victor and Edith Turner (1969; 1974; 1978; 1985) made the provocative suggestion that the behaviour exemplified in rites of passage could be understood as a microcosm of something that was also happening on a larger, macrocosmic scale. If peoples of old needed the liminal experience, so do all human beings, and the creative imagination has evoked ways and means of articulating and facilitating this need. To substantiate their claim the Turners visited and participated in pilgrimages all over the world. There is some-

50

thing universal in the notion of *pilgrimage*, and whether it happens at Lourdes, Mecca, Jerusalem, or Amritsar, there are underlying subconscious features, confirming universal yearnings of the human heart.

At a conscious level, people go on pilgrimages for a range of reasons: in gratitude for blessings received; to repent for wrongdoing; to beseech God's help in time of need, or simply as a test of endurance. And we all assume that the choice to go on pilgrimage is that of a specific individual or group of people. We also assume that the benefits reaped are exclusive to those who participated in the experience.

At the *subconscious* level, a great deal more is taking place. The pilgrims are 'sent' (missioned) by the whole people, and the benefits they reap individually also have communal benefit for those who 'sent' them. The pilgrims themselves are somehow changed, but that change has a ripple effect right through the community of which they are a part.

Reflecting on *how* this might be possible – because the *why* can only be understood in a spiritual (faith) context – eventually led the Turners to a deeper comprehension of the nature of liminality. While exploring the pilgrimage experience in various parts of the world the Turners frequently encountered the monastic and religious life. Is this also a universal phenomenon, they began to ask, and if so, why? Could this be another expression of the universal desire for liminal witness and experience? Perhaps this is the crucial element with the aid of which all the other noted phenomena can be better understood![6]

In the early 1980s, the Turners concluded that the monastic/religious (vowed) Life was the core mediation of the human need for liminal experience. Through the vowed life, people in general seek to explore and articulate those deeper universal values to which we all aspire. Consequently, we find versions of the vowed life in all the great religions, but, more importantly, we find attempts at incarnating the deeper (archetypal) values in all cultures

51

known to humankind, many predating the era of major religions by thousands of years.

Subconscious processes rarely are mediated in manageable, rational ways. Even at a personal level, breakthrough often happens through crisis or breakdown. We find a similar orientation on a universal scale: *paradox* is the norm, rather than the exception.

To understand the human need for liminality and its universal mediation through the vowed life (which is not the only mode although it does seem to have primary significance) we need to be able to engage – spiritually, mentally and factually -with the notion of *paradox*. In that way, we begin to comprehend the incomprehensible; we are enabled to hold apparent contradictions; we outgrow the masculine urge to dominate and control; we no longer need totally rational explanations; we begin to feel at home within the mystery that surrounds us.

Creating the liminal groups

The process which generates liminality comes from deep within the human subconscious; more accurately, from deep within the collective consciousness of humanity (or what the Jungians call the collective unconscious). What seems to be happening is this: we humans call forth some members of our species, and we push them towards a marginal threshold, wherein we invite them to live out more deeply on *our* behalf (not on *their own* behalf) those deeper values we cherish and admire innately.

At this juncture some concrete examples may be helpful. Because the vowed life in the West is so institutionalised and conformed into the mainstream culture, it has lost practically all semblance of a liminal movement. In the East, things are not a great deal better, although one encounters some compelling and inspiring examples. One notes, in the tradition of Theravada Buddhism, the custom of every young man spending some time in the monastery;

it can range from a number of months to a number of years. When a young lady informs her parents about her lover, prior to her parents enquiring about his family background, his character, his wealth, job, etc., they are likely to ask first and foremost: how much time has he spent in the monastery? From this they will gauge his *maturity* (not necessarily his holiness) and hence his suitability as a partner for their daughter.

In that same tradition, as in the East generally, it is the people who recruit for the monastery, and not the monks (religious) themselves, as in the West. At a subconscious level, the people intuit that the monastery is essential to their culture and well-being. It is the *value-radiation centre*, in which there are constellated the deeper dreams and aspirations of the surrounding culture. Consequently, in some far eastern countries, such as Thailand and Burma, people will consult monks about commerce, finances, politics, medicine, law, etc. The monastic person does not have to be an expert in all or any of these fields. What is being sought is a quality of wisdom that goes much deeper than factual information.

Some years ago I met a self-confessed atheist spending a few quiet days at a Catholic monastery in England. He told me he had been visiting the monastery for over 20 years. To my question, 'Why do you come here?' most people would respond: 'to have some peace and quiet', 'to pray', 'to consult a monk', 'to share in the worship'. But my atheist friend gave a somewhat different response with distinctive echoes of liminal vision: 'There is something here that is important to me and I need to connect with it every now and again'. I wish to suggest that this 'vague' response is a great deal more authentic than the clearer and more predictable statements other respondents are likely to make.

Although we ourselves have 'created' the liminal group (or people), at a *conscious* level we will exhibit a whole range of feelings towards the liminars. We may deeply admire and cherish them – this tends to be a temporary response. We may find them threatening and too challenging – in which case we will begin to punish, persecute and even execute them. We may feel ambivalent or indifferent towards them – usually because they are no longer genuinely liminal, in which case we will substitute a more dynamic replacement. We are never at ease with our liminal people. Their purpose is not to put us at ease, but to jolt us continually into a fuller sense of life.

As I write these words I am reminded how Chittister (1994 p. 103) challenges religious to reclaim their prophetic vocation:

> It is our turn now... to be willing to be strangers in our own land, to be willing to stay where we do not fit, to be committed to say what is not welcome, to be heard, so that creation does not go on creating in vain. It is our turn now to speak a prophet's word on behalf of those who have no voice but ours. It is our turn now to gamble with our lives so that others may live.

The vocation to liminality comes from the people rather than from within the liminar himself/herself. For Christians this may be a disturbing notion, since we associate *vocation* exclusively with God's mysterious workings in human life. What is at stake here, I suggest, is our understanding of how God works in people and in the world generally. As Christians, we believe in an incarnational God who works primarily through the creative process of people and planet, and consequently, co-creates with the people. In this sense, there is no conflict between the divine and the human. If anything, the call to listen and respond more responsibly to the divine urgings is increased and not diminished.

There exists, therefore, an unceasing interplay between the divine and human co-creativity. Innately we humans perpetually co-create towards greater value-radiation. Our innate yearning for the fullness of life is what drives us to do this. And one of the intriguing paradoxical outcomes is the upsurge of liminal groups of which the monastic/ religious life seems to be the supreme expression.

What happens, therefore, when the orders and congregations no longer serve in a genuinely liminal way, as is largely the case today? Presumably, the groups either reclaim their liminal role or become extinct. But is it as simple as that? Is it even appropriate for those groups to seek to perpetuate their own existence? Surely that is a matter for the people, and for the divine-human co-creativity which calls the groups into being in the first place, and presumably will regenerate such groups if they are open to serve in the novel capacity evoked by the fresh requirements of each new cultural era. For such groups survival cannot be an issue; service is what they are all about.

We recall once more, that the task of the liminal group is the mediation of universally shared values. The values seem to remain essentially the same, but their mediation and application demands fresh expression at the different moments of time and culture. Although the monastic/religious life seems to be the primary mode of mediation, it does not necessarily have to be so, in which case the co-creative consciousness will bring into being other groups and movements to serve the liminal function.

Liminality is *always* at work in our world and if the official liminars, the orders and congregations fail in their task then other groups will be invoked into being. They may not be distinctly *religious* in nature; they do not have to be. At the present time a number of 'secular' groups seem to be serving this purpose, in a way that engages our attention and evokes our response. These include, particularly, *feminist* groups and *ecology* groups. The former articulate the demise of patriarchal values and the need to reclaim the long suppressed feminine values; the latter recall us to our essential bond with creation and to the need to realign our energies and resources with the sacred unfolding of creation itself. Both groups offer a contemporary cutting edge for values long subverted, that are being invoked afresh in our world today.

Greenpeace provides a timely example of a contemporary liminal movement. It serves as a type of conscience for the planet. Few can deny the *deep truth* it seeks to highlight and promote yet many people *consciously* dismiss and denounce it. Its activities evoke both anger and admiration. Its way of doing things – like that of the ancient prophets – is paradoxically different from the 'norm' and its members take enormous risks with their lives and well-being. Like the ascetics of bygone days, they are prepared to sacrifice everything for the cause to which they are committed. They may not be religious in any formal sense, but few can deny the deep spiritual significance of their lives and actions, although they themselves may not be consciously aware of this.

Many of today's alternative movements exhibit the liminal challenge much more powerfully and coherently than the formal liminars. Wholistic health movements, alternative technologies, workers' co-operatives, base communities, attempts at ethical investment, and attempts at discerning alternative socio-economic and political strategies are all endowed with liminal potential. These are the challenging and disturbing voices of our time; they keep alive on behalf of humanity the liminal cutting edge.

At an international conference on religious life held in Rome in the autumn of 1993 one speaker referred to 'secular' and 'sacred' liminality. This dualistic distinction is not operative at the deeply subconscious level. This is a projection of our conscious mind, which seeks to divide (and conquer) into convenient, but superficial, opposites. It is the *unity* of life rather than its fragmentation into dualistic opposites that concerns the liminal vocation. At this level everything is sacred; all aspirations are of the heart that yearns for what is truly life-giving.

Liminality thrives on imagination and creativity. To that extent, it serves a complementary role to our human patriarchal urge to structure and control in a logical, rational way. In the long tradition of the monastic/religious life, the 'interior' life tends to take priority. For the major

56

religions interiority is frequently juxtaposed with external action or behaviour, the affairs of the so-called secular domain. But the tradition of the interior contemplative life serves a deeper, more wholistic purpose, based on a more ancient tradition: the desire to safeguard and foster the intuitive, the imagination, the feminine, the spiritual as the fundamental layer of all reality, animate and inanimate alike. These are the values that motivate and sustain all liminal groups.

The Turners often equate liminality with *communitas* (sometimes described as *anti-structure*). Although liminality is often illustrated through the behaviour of individual people, it is essentially a *communal* phenomenon. It is brought into being from the *collective* consciousness of all humanity, not on the instigation of a few spiritually enlightened beings. Its form of mediation, although focusing on specific persons, is predominantly communal; even Van Gennep sensed this strong communitarian influence. And its overall purpose is to effect change on a *communal* scale. Quite rightly, Hobbs (1985 p. 139) suggests that the task of the prophetic liminal group is to concentrate not on social *structure*, but on social *change*.

As noted in earlier chapters religious life in its origins, is often assumed to be predominantly eremitical. But this view has never been accepted fully, and, among monastic writers, the tendency in recent years is to highlight and reclaim the communal forms which co-existed with the eremitical expression and were probably a great deal more widespread. To some extent the eremitical individualistic focus seems to have been rooted in a spirituality of the *wilderness* (desert) modelled on Jesus' own 40 days of endurance with the forces of evil. But the interpretation of this experience is a great deal more complex than many scholars allow for (see Kittel 1964; Fisher 1989 pp. 192-195).

The desire to be in communion meaningfully with significant others is a major issue of our times: personally, interpersonally, politically and globally. The robust individualism which still features strongly in western culture is an aberration of patriarchal times, one that has little to offer for the future well-being of person or planet. Inter-relatedness is the fundamental nature of all life-forms, and serves as a core value of every liminal enterprise.

The vows as liminal values

In so far as religious life today is intended to provide the liminal ambience for our culture and for our world, the underlying value system is embodied primarily in the three vows traditionally named celibacy, poverty and obedience. Even the very language of the vows diminishes their potential for value-radiation. The emphasis rests heavily on renunciation, denial, suppression, deprivation and denunciation of the surrounding culture. As currently understood and lived, the vows do not foster a counter-culture, but an *anti*-culture.

Underlying the vowed life in all the major world religions is an anti-world, ascetical polemic. We misinterpret the deeper meaning of the vows because we begin with a faulty cosmology, which modern writers like Fiand (1990 pp. 7-33) and Merkle (1992 pp. 93-100) strive to set aright. With the rise of the Agricultural Revolution, we humans set out to conquer the world; when that failed, we projected onto the universe our negative and derisory feelings. We set up the cosmos as an alien force, with which we began to wage apocalyptic warfare. If we couldn't conquer it our *man-made* God could, and *he* would do so in a treacherous and mighty way (hence the-end-of-the-world polemic in all the major religions). This anti-world spirituality with its accompanying asceticism of renouncing all bodily and earthly goods, became the overriding concern for the mo-nastic/religious life, affecting in a particularly deleterious way the meaning and significance of the three vows.

In the ascetical frame of reference the three vows de-note renunciation of: the body, sexuality, procreativity and pleasure (celibacy); material goods, money, possessions (poverty); domination, control and will-power (obedience). Underpinning the ascetical rationale is a more ancient *aesthetical* strand wherein counter-cultural *values* become much more apparent. In this context *celibacy* is the invitation to name, clarify and mediate the changing sexual and relational issues of human intimacy; the liminal group or person holds the paradoxes, tensions and possibilities which the people at large realise only partially in their lived experience. The task of the liminal celibate is not about getting it all right, but about facilitating a process of exploration and growth that leads towards authentic personhood and meaningful life-giving relationships. I suggest, therefore, that we rename this the vow for *Relatedness*.

Poverty, in its popular connotation, is the abandonment of all material possessions, so that one can move towards God untrammelled by earthly attachments. In its liminal counter-cultural context, poverty (which I suggest we rename the vow for *Stewardship)* becomes a call to engagement, rather than one of disengagement: to engage with all the goods of creation, promoting a sense of *relating* to them, rather than conquering or controlling them; fostering a mutually interdependent use of all things entrusted to human care, and promulgating stewardship as the dominant orientation towards the goods of creation. In this case, as with all the vows, instead of being a measuring rod for individual spiritual growth, the vow takes on ecological and global applications.

Obedience carries connotations of subservience and passivity. It is intended to be a virtue that enables and facilitates a fair distribution of power in a hierarchically-structured mode. In practice, it often led to a perception of the one offering obedience having to abrogate conscious choices and submit completely to another human being, whose understanding and knowledge were equated to those of God. In its deeper liminal meaning, obedience may be renamed as the vow for *Partnership*, inviting the devotee to engage with issues of power; to name the oppression and

59

sin of power; to confront and disempower sinful structures and systems; to empower the powerless, by inculcating values of sharing and participating in issues of power, and in decision making. The goal of such a process is based on the conviction that we are all co-responsible for our shared power to be co-creators with God in the world.

By reframing the vows so that we focus on *values of engagement*, rather than on *laws of disengagement*, we can comprehend more clearly the role and function of the liminal group. (The pastoral and practical implications will be dealt with in chapter six.) A first point of major importance is that the liminal group does not exist for its own sake, nor for its self-perpetuation, but for the sake of the people. Its role is to serve and service the needs of others. In the post-Reformation Christian Church, the theology of religious life focused on the pursuit of perfection. Religious were to become specialists in holiness, so that the cumulative effects of their sanctity would enable the whole Church to attain the perfection of heaven, understood, in the cosmology of the time, to be outside and beyond this world. Although the pursuit of perfection was intended as something larger than the religious life itself, it quickly became an incestuous ego-trip on the perfection of the self and the salvation of one's individual soul. This introverted, Jansenistic spirituality, although no longer formally propagated, has still a significant following among religious women and men of our time.

Liminality in no sense involves an escape from earthly or human reality. Quite the opposite! Liminality, of its very nature seeks to engage with real issues confronting people and the planet in the key relational areas of their lives especially in reference to pleasure (relatedness), property (stewardship) and power (partnership). In so far as the liminal vocation pursues ultimate meanings, and seeks to explore and articulate the deeper aspirations of the human heart, then it is spiritual in the full sense of the word (which includes *secularity*). It may not be distinctly *religious* in terms of allegiance to one or other – or any – religious

system. Liminality does not need formal religion to validate its existence, nor to justify its *modus operandi*. It is
fundamentally *spiritual* in all its modes and operations, but
not necessarily religious in any formal sense.

Accountable to Whom?

To whom, therefore, are the liminars accountable? Ultimately to those who brought them into being: that is, the
people (*laos*) and, through the people, God, with whom the
liminars are called in a unique – but not superior – way to
be co-creators. How this accountability is to be exercised is
largely an unexplored question. Accountability to the Church
(in the case of Christian religious) or to the official religion
(in the case of non-Christian forms) confines the vowed
life to a formal religious structure which almost totally
negates its liminal and prophetic meaning. In terms of both
support and understanding, the formal ecclesiastical and
religious structures rarely provide a challenging or inspiring affirmation.

In contemporary Christianity, religious life is swamped
by oppressive, antagonistic legalism, that destroys any hope
of open, creative dialogue with the Church. Little wonder
that many contemporary religious are exploring and con-
sidering *non-canonical* status. On the other hand, the
Tariqahs of Islam, because they are perceived to be too
mystical (and, therefore, a threat to the rather rigid legal
requirements of that faith), tend to be conveniently ignored; most written works on the Islamic faith do not even
refer to the Tariqahs. Universally, religious encounter a
great deal of ignorance and fear from formal religious
institutions.

Perhaps the model of accountability to be explored is
somewhat akin to the prophetic movement of the Old
Testament. In conjunction with the common people, the
prophet considered himself/herself a full socio-political
citizen, subject to the king as the formal mediator of the

'secular' and 'sacred' values. But the prophet clearly understood himself/herself to be different from the people (a dimension of the prophetic vocation that none of the prophets particularly cherished), and set in a counter-cultural relationship with the king and the official *status-quo* which he represented. In word and action, the prophet challenged and confronted the royal power, especially when it deviated from serving genuine human need and focused instead on its own perpetuation. But the prophetic person also assumed (subconsciously, it seemed) a higher authority; frequently reminding the king that he is ultimately accountable to God, from whom all authority emanates. Here we have the double element of accountability to both God and the people.

Many parallels exist between the liminal and prophetic vocations, which in turn resemble the calling of the shaman and other sacred personages of prehistoric times. The tendency in contemporary spirituality is to over-spiritualise these figures and to that degree strip them of their potential to be catalysts at the cutting edge. Their vocation is to occupy the marginal spaces and articulate on behalf of humanity those divinely-endowed values through which we attain our fullness as creatures of God – and co-creators with God – in the unfolding dance of creation.

Liminality touches not merely on the deep story (and structure) of religious life, but also names a central experience of numerous people in today's world. As waves of change shake traditional foundations and stretch or dismantle traditional parameters, many people feel uprooted, dislocated and often pushed to the edge. The liminal threshold of today's world is densely populated, frequently by people who are confused, lost and lonely. The answers of yesterday's gurus neither enlighten nor reassure. A new wisdom is needed for our time, and nobody should be better equipped to provide it than those whose whole life is about living in the liminal spaces.

The more we religious move to the frontiers the more we become catalysts for change; the quicker we learn to dance to a different tune then the sooner we will respond afresh to the spiritual and cultural hunger of our time. Not only will we have reframed religious life itself; more importantly, we will have helped to name the transformation that is taking place and empowered people to engage with growth and change – and in that way contribute to a new lease of life for our planet and for all its life-forms.

CHAPTER FOUR

The theological frame: Expanding traditional horizons

Theology is never a final, finished statement, but always a provisional and ongoing process, because of its situated perspective in history and because of its limited nature as a knowledge of God... The Kingdom of God serves as a focal referent for interpreting the diversity and the constancy of how God acts in history.

Rebecca S. Chopp

Theology is a Christian concept, described by St Anselm as faith seeking understanding, and by Paul Tillich as the ultimate concern about the ground and meaning of our being. Theology has been, largely, a deductive science, beginning with the reality of God as depicted in the scriptures and mediated through the Christian tradition of the past 2,000 years. For mainstream theology the formal revelation of God to humanity ends with the New Testament (or, more precisely, with the death of the last apostle). From there on, its meaning is mediated under the guided authorization of the Church as the official guardian of Christian orthodoxy. Christian theology, in this sense, is very much the creation of the institutionalised Church.

For much of the Christian era, the Bible was taken literally and at its face value. Only in the nineteenth century did biblical exegesis – and the freedom to interpret – come into vogue. With it, the face and function of theology began to change, from a science offering ultimate answers to one which formulates and explores ultimate questions.

Currently two dominant strands co-exist. The first, and by far the most prevalent, can be dated approximately from

1563 CE (the end of the Council of Trent) to 1963 (the Second Vatican Council). The post-Tridentine era was characterised by a Church desperately trying to hold its superior position of the high Middle Ages, and setting itself up as an adversary to all movements which *it* considered alien to the Christian gospel. From this arrogant and defensive position it added new edge to the slogan: 'Outside the Church there's no salvation'. One could argue that, during this epoch there was no theology other than ecclesiology.

The second epoch from 1960 onwards, is where the theological enterprise begins to stretch the frontiers of what had become a closed ecclesiastical system. Once more theology began to look beyond the Church to the world (this is exemplified particularly in the promulgation of *Gaudium et Spes* at Vatican II). In fact, theology began to break loose from the theological tradition of some 1,900 years, and instead of taking the Gospels and the revealed tradition as its starting-point, theologians began with the *lived experience* of people, especially the poor and marginalised, and used that experiential base as the foundation stone for theological reflection (e.g., liberation theology and feminist theology).

Engaging with the new cosmology

The major difference between these two approaches is not in the theology, but in the *cosmology* (see diagram on p. 66). The vision of Trent was fundamentally a world-denouncing one, in which creation is viewed as deficient, impermanent, transitory, prone to evil and something not to be taken seriously; the real life is not here, but hereafter. Heaven is the perfect place and it exists outside and beyond this creation. At best creation was viewed as a necessary stage for us humans to pass through on our way to eternity. Accompanying this cosmology is an anthropology (or, more accurately, an anthropomorphism) which in conjunction with classical science, deems human intelligence at this

THE THEOLOGICAL FRAME

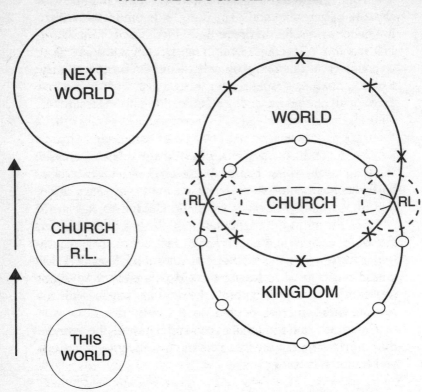

This diagram illustrates the theological shift under consideration. On the left are three closed, independent circles, the largest representing the 'next world' or the afterlife considered to be eternal and the place of ultimate fulfilment; the smallest, 'this world', considered to be materialistic, imperfect, transitory and not to be taken seriously. Represented in the centre is the Church as organisation; with the monopoly of salvation, it alone can get people from this world to the next. And within the Church circle is Religious Life (R.L.) considered to have the monopoly of perfection. In this representation on the left, theology, which is the preserve of the Church, is considered to be the queen of the sciences.

On the right, all aspects of the diagram are open, interconnected and movement is multidirectional. There is ONE world, namely the expanding, complex universe which modern cosmology is only beginning to comprehend. Of equal size is the circle marked *Kingdom*, the biblical concept explored at length in this chapter. The *Church* serves as a bridge between World and Kingdom in the sense that the Church is called to be the servant and herald of the Kingdom in the World. Religious Life is relocated at the primary points of intersection between World and Kingdom, referred to in this book as the liminal spaces. In this diagram, *cosmology* rather than *theology* becomes the queen of the sciences.

66

stage of evolution to be insurmountable: the human mind is capable of grasping and explaining ultimate truths – theological or scientific – and, in time, the *human understanding* becomes *God-like dogma*. Humans begin to play God; an accusation we rightly direct at the scientific community, while turning a blind eye to the fact that such behaviour exists with equal virulence in the theological community as well.

In the mid-twentieth century a new cosmology began to unfold – one that is still in the making – a new global vision, which as yet has not impinged upon the overall awareness of the human community. In the new cosmology the creative energy comes from within, rather than from without. God does not create as if he is an external agent, the *deus ex machina* of classical science, but in a divine-human engagement of co-creativity. And humans have acquired a different self-understanding (anthropology), not as *masters* of creation, but *co-creators*, striving to cooperate with our creative God.

Creation is fundamentally good as it unfolds in its complex life-giving trajectory. Nothing is external to the co-creative evolutionary process. It is all we have and everything we have. We make it our heaven or our hell, depending on how we learn to live interdependently with its prodigious array of life-forms. In this new global ambience, the task of theology is to engage with the lived experience of both *person* and *planet*, and to articulate the divine-human story, forever unfolding around us. The task of the theologian today is to be a listener for the ever new revelation of the divine-human co-creative process.

The task of the Church in this new theological ambience is to be the community that celebrates what the creative Spirit is doing in our midst. Nurture and healing are two of the chief ecclesiological tasks as depicted in the Christian notion of sacrament; with the Church herself as the sacramental sign *par excellence* as *Lumen Gentium* (1) enunciates.

One of the major problems confronting religious life

67

today is its theological depravity. According to Thomas Aquinas the purpose of the vowed life is the pursuit of *perfect charity*; a description that still merits serious attention and consideration. The post-Tridentine tradition took that description and effectively de-Christianised it. For the pursuit of *perfect charity* it substituted the pursuit of *perfection*. The *charity* was eliminated; heroic ascetical achievement became the new criterion for holiness and salvation. That deviant development and the ensuing theology – if it can be called theology at all – still provides the spiritual context for the vowed life. Even the Second Vatican Council failed to revamp a theology for religious life as it attempted to do for other aspects of Christian (Catholic) life today.

Reframing the theological context remains one of the major challenges confronting contemporary religious. Faced with the new cosmology, we no longer flee nor abandon the world. That same world calls us forth, and invites us to engage with it and with one another in ways that are largely unexplored. Without a solid theological undergirding, our vision and task as religious is largely incomplete.

In the reframing task we begin where contemporary theology encourages us to begin: with our *lived experience*. In its present context that is largely polarized between, on the one hand, the death and diminution of the post-Tridentine model, which still has a substantial following; and, on the other hand, the many attempts since the Second Vatican Council to renew and reform the monastic/religious life. Rather than become embroiled in these polarized and divisive ideologies (which I acknowledge are currently a major aspect of the lived experience), I choose to move into the deeper experiential layers of the vowed life as lived out universally, especially in the other great religions and from within the rich resources of prehistoric times. And I focus particularly on the liminal prophetic dimension, which underpins the vowed life, as primarily countercultural.

As noted in previous chapters the liminal focus is on values and their mediation through life-giving relationships. It is this focus on *relationships* that opens up a new theological horizon, as relevant to the Church and to the world as it is to the religious life itself. I refer to what the Gospels call the *Kingdom of God*, often referred to in contemporary scholarship as the *New Reign of God*.

Kingdom and Church

In the story of Christian theology special concern about the person of Jesus emerges at an early stage. Already in the third and fourth centuries debate about the *nature* of Jesus, especially his divinity – which was the primary concern of the Councils of Nicaea and Chalcedon – gave Christian theology a distinctive orientation. The *person* of Jesus became the focus for prayer, morality, religious observance and theological discourse to such a degree that the *mission* of Jesus was largely overlooked. Various attempts to address this imbalance ensued in subsequent centuries; the least satisfactory being the post-Tridentine development of attributing the mission of Jesus not just primarily but exclusively to the Church. (Hence the revival of the dictum, initially used by Cyprian and Origen: 'Outside the Church there is no salvation.') Contemporary theology, especially since the 1960s, struggles to redress this balance, and in the process of doing so has to engage with profound questions of its own meaning and relevance for the world of our time (see the pioneering work of Fuellenbach 1995).

In the Gospels we cannot separate the *person* and *mission* of Jesus. The one only makes sense through the other. Everything Jesus is and stands for is intertwined with the vision of the new reality dawning upon the world: a new presence of God among the people that declares defunct the old ways of relating to reality – especially through the patriarchal hierarchy governing and determining life from the top downwards – evoking a novel set of relationships

69

marked by justice, love, peace and liberation. The Gospels call this new way of being in the world 'the Kingdom of God' or the more inclusive term *New Reign of God* which I propose to use for the rest of this chapter.

It is disturbing for many Christians to learn that apparently Jesus was not particularly interested in a *church*. In the four Gospels there are only *three* references to church (all in Matthew's Gospel) and biblical scholars are far from agreed on what these texts mean. On the other hand, there are over 120 references to the New Reign of God, which was quite unambiguously the primary preoccupation and concern of Jesus.

The emphasis already begins to change when we move to the Acts of the Apostles and the Pauline literature, but for much of the early Christian epoch a sense prevailed that the role of the Church is to be the *servant* and *herald* of the New Reign of God. It is in the community of the believers that the agenda of the New Reign should have continued most clearly and strongly. But in a short time the Church, like its secular counterparts, became preoccupied with its own survival and growth; correspondingly, it lost sight of its central function and purpose – to be the primary agent for the unfolding of God's New Reign. This aberrant development has become particularly acute in our own time.[7] To recall the Church to its primary task would seem to be one of the chief prophetic challenges of religious life today.

Gospel references to the New Reign are immensely diverse and complex in nature. We are never offered a *definition* of the New Reign, and the several descriptions use the narrative infrastructure of the parables or the symbolic format of the miracles. What is clear is that the New Reign transcends the mores and values of all the other 'reigns' that dominated the culture of the time, the chief one being that of the royal figure of the king or emperor. On only one occasion in the synoptic Gospels does Jesus allow himself to be called 'king' – on the final journey to Jerusalem; here, symbolic action speaks louder than anywhere else in the New Testament. As a king, Jesus should be riding on the royal beast of domination and warfare, namely the *horse*; instead he rides on a *donkey*, the beast of burden dear to the ordinary people. Here kingly power is turned on its head; it is openly and provocatively declared to be totally alien to the Christian process.

Consequently the New Reign is characterised by radical equality and inclusiveness. Even the earth itself is included in the new vision (Matt 5:5). By the same token the New Reign assumes global proportions – there is nothing in the Gospels to suggest that it is for Christians only, quite the opposite – it embraces horizons that include all peoples and cultures within a time-scale that extends into the open-ended future (which the Church later interpreted as being about the *afterlife*; but the Gospels never equate this with the New Reign). The New Reign is embodied in a special way in the life and ministry of Jesus: but everyone is invited to *participate* in the work of the vineyard (cf. Matt 20:1-16), in the co-creative unfolding of the new era that is being proclaimed perhaps nowhere more succinctly than in the oft-quoted words from Revelation 21:5: 'Behold I make all things new'.

To facilitate a more creative exploration of this core truth of our Christian faith I offer a definition which, hope-fully, will not constrict our vision, but will be sufficiently porous and inclusive to do justice to its central meaning. The New Reign may be described as *a new world order, marked by right relationships of justice, love, peace and liberation*. At the heart of this vision is the notion of *right relationships*. Old patriarchal ways of relating – which still dominate our contemporary world – are declared irrelevant and inappropriate for the committed Christian. And the ambience of such relationships is not just among people, but with all elements of creation, including planet earth, the cosmos and the divine source of all that exists (irrespective of what name we use).

The reader will notice the frequent use of the word *new*. There is something radically new in what Jesus was about, considered by one scholar (Sheehan 1986) to be the abolition of *all* religion so that we can rediscover our relationship with God within the process of *creation* itself. In the popular tradition of the Christian Church, and indeed in all the major religious systems, the safeguarding and preservation of the *old* takes precedence over the fostering and promotion of the *new*. Obviously Jesus did cherish his inheritance and traditions, but the Gospels offer an unambiguous invitation to outgrow past traditions and paradigms no matter how sacred or solemnized by time. As Christians we are invited to be a people ever fresh, vital and attuned to the ever-new stirrings of the Spirit. Herein lies a unique prophetic challenge for us religious.

Throughout the entire post-Reformation era the dominant frame of reference for religious life was the *Church as institution*. Within that context religious were expected to be loyal and obedient servants, whose role was to be specialists in the way of perfection providing a model of holiness that the whole Church could emulate – one that would guarantee eternal salvation in the world to come. In this ecclesiastical culture and its accompanying cosmology the New Reign of God was almost completely subverted and like everybody else, religious ended up being functionaries of an institution that had largely lost its way.

It is this closed misguided institution that began to disintegrate (from internal malaise rather than from external attack) in the 1950s, and that Pope John XXIII sought to redress by convening the Second Vatican Council in the early 1960s. The conscious hope of the Council was to instigate a process of reform, hopefully without too much disruption. But the internal decay was so deep-seated and pervasive that only those with a profound sense of history could understand what began to transpire and what has ensued over subsequent decades.

Since 1960 we have been witnessing the disintegration of a mighty ecclesiastical empire that had deviated quite seriously from the vision of God's New Reign; a monolith that may have to collapse entirely (over the next few centuries) before a Church *at the service of the New Reign* arises from the dying embers of the old. And herein may be a supreme challenge to us religious: can we accept the inevitability and necessity of *our dying*, engage with it in a truly paschal way and integrate it as a precondition for resurrection hope? In that way we can offer to the Church (and to the many other patriarchal institutions facing decline and disintegration at this time) a model for transcending *denial*, gracefully dying to its past and courageously opening itself to the new future of the creative Spirit.

If we Religious are to reclaim our liminal prophetic role – which belongs to the New Reign much more integrally than to the Church – then a process of disengagement from the institutional Church is both desirable and necessary. This is one of the most painful and dislocating aspects of the reframing we explore in the present work. It may be salutary to remind ourselves of those moments in the sacred story of our orders and congregations in which some founders and many foundresses had to confront the hierarchical Church, often to the point of open conflict, in order to bring to birth their creative and prophetic dreams. Nor should we forget the eminent apostolic endeavours of many religious, often veering far outside and beyond the official boundaries imposed by the Church. I do not wish to advocate conflict for its own sake. My contention is that we religious can no longer shy away from the theological reframing suggested in this chapter: that our primary allegiance is to the New Reign, and not to the institutional Church; and that we must not diminish our commitment to the former in order to remain loyal to the latter.

Every aspect of reframing explored in this book reconnects us with deeper, more ancient, and more authentic traditions, which comprise our true uniqueness as a liminal prophetic movement. If we are to be true to our mission and to the *entire* people of God to whom we are sent (only a small proportion of whom belong to the Church) then we have little choice but to face the painful and challenging decisions that confront us at this time.

Religious today are invited to become 'Kingdom spotters'. This means confronting, contesting and even denouncing those systems and institutions which militate against the values of the New Reign; many of our brothers and sisters in Central and Latin America have given their lives in this very task. On the other hand religious of the western world tend to collude with those systems which oppress the peoples of the southern hemisphere. Our lifestyle and value-appropriation emulates that of the dominant culture, and apostolically only a few among us openly challenge and denounce our oppressively sinful structures. A sizeable proportion of religious still participate in a western educational system which openly inculcates capitalistic competitive values, which are clearly at variance with the values of the New Reign.

As 'Kingdom spotters' we fall well short of the call to confront, protest against and denounce those systems and structures which undermine the values of the Gospel. Sadly, we are even more incoherent in naming and celebrating the upsurge of those values in the many contemporary movements of the Spirit, especially those taking place outside the formal churches and religions. I refer in particular to the ecological and feminist consciousness with their accompanying sense of hope and vitality, along with the several small, often unnoticed efforts to create a more just and humane world.

Because of our close liaison with the hierarchical Church of the post-Tridentine era, we religious devote much energy and resourcefulness to canonical rectitude. When confronted by the urgent call of our times we often hesitate and look over our shoulder to see if what we know in our hearts we should do will be acceptable to the bishop, the parish priest, or the patriarchal guardians of the health or educational services. We have largely lost the daring subversive vision of the prophets, old and more recent; we have largely betrayed our liminal calling to be catalysts for new possibilities that will express and articulate afresh those deeper values to which the people aspire.

These values are identical to those of God's New Reign as embodied and proclaimed by Jesus. Striving to follow this vision is congruent with our liminal vocation and our prophetic call. It is noteworthy that practically every time Jesus is confronted and challenged in his provocative ministry (especially in those moments of parabolic narrative and miracle enactment) he justifies and defends his actions by invoking the prophetic message of the Old Testament. The life and message of Jesus is rooted quite unambiguously in the prophetic tradition. Ours should be also if we stand any hope of engaging meaningfully with the world of our time.

As already noted, the creation and formation of *right relationships* forms the heart of God's New Reign. And it is not merely relationships between people, but the very capacity to relate which seems to be the fundamental essence of nature, on the one hand, and of the Godhead, on the other. Particle physics and the ongoing developments of the quantum theory illustrate coherently and convincingly that *relationships* are much more fundamental to the subatomic structure of the universe than the long-sought isolated building blocks. Life, it appears, does not consist of discrete isolated entities of which everything is constituted, but of interrelating patterns of energy that ceaselessly intertwine and interweave in the perpetual process of co-creation.

At the other end of the spectrum, there exists a long tradition of perceiving God not as an isolated individual person but as an interrelating community of three – what in the Christian tradition we call the *Trinity*. We find versions of such trinitarian allusions to godhead in practically all the major religions; more significantly, we find a similar understanding of the divine nature in prehistoric goddess worship dating back to 40,000 BCE. What we are encountering here, I suggest, is not some profound religious dogma, but an archetypal truth that people have felt in their hearts for millennia, a deep inner wisdom that informs the creative imagination about the nature of God as first and

75

foremost a *capacity for relatedness*. In other words, our trinitarian doctrines are human efforts at naming God's real essence and the nearest we can hope to come – which is probably a profoundly authentic insight – is that our God is above all else, a power for relatedness.

The capacity to relate, therefore seems to be the fundamental essence of the cosmos as revealed through contemporary science (the micro level), but also the fundamental nature of God (the macro level). It is also the central ingredient of God's New Reign and, one has good reason to assume, the fundamental aspiration of all religion and spirituality. Very rightly, therefore, Zappone (1991) describes *spirituality* as the relational component of lived experience; and the discernment of such experience is what often leads to a search for genuine *community*. The Christian Church proffers the creation and development of community as its fundamental *raison d'etre*, as indeed do all the major religions in a range of different ways.

Community as centre

The monastic and religious life today struggles to reclaim *community* as a key value. Consciously this is an attempt at a more supportive and discerning ambience, but in the light of the above considerations we can see that there are unconscious considerations of enormously rich and complex impact. Little wonder that community can be such an attractive and yet contentious issue for so many religious today (cf. Fiand 1992).

Our theological praxis, therefore, is about the creation of community structures wherein we explore, negotiate and mediate those values which realign our lives with the 'heart centre' of creation itself. This 'centre' is the capacity to relate, whether understood microscopically or macroscopically. In this vision the old dualistic barriers between the divine and the human disintegrate, and we begin to engage with life in its essential vitality and unity. For religious, therefore, community is a great deal more than a specific living arrangement. It is first and foremost a theological fact, because we have been overtaken by God's New Reign and we are missioned to live out and promote that deeper quality of interrelatedness through which we become a liminal presence for all people. The pastoral implications of this challenge we explore in chapter six.

At the beginning of this chapter we indicated that our renewed cosmology requires a whole new way of doing theology, not over against the world in adversarial antagonism, but in dialogue with our world, striving to be ever-listening and receptive to the divine disclosures. Theology is faced with something of a quantum leap with ramifications for religious life as well as for all other areas of living reality.

It is no longer adequate to formulate a theology of the vowed life around an exclusive pursuit of perfection over against an imperfect world, nor is it appropriate to build a theology on the notion of religious life as an eschatological sign (cf. *Lumen Gentium* 44). This maintains a focus on fulfilment in a world to come, diverting serious attention from the one world which we believe to be the locus of God's co-creativity – past, present and future. Religious life is not about values pertaining to a life hereafter; rather, its vocation is to address the challenge and struggle to live openly, creatively and responsibly in the here and now of our planetary and cosmic ambience. We are not meant to be a supernatural sign pointing beyond the incompleteness of the present order to the fulfilment of a life to come. Our mission is to be at the heart of creation in what we now understand to be *one* world (of which the afterlife is one dimension), providing a liminal witness to those values which endure – into that fullness of life which we yearn for in our hearts.

According to the 1981 Vatican document *Religious and Human Advancement* (24), religious are invited to become *signs of communion* for the world. The call to engage with those deep values which constitute our liminal witness is only possible in a communitarian ambience. Only in communion with significant others – whether within a specific order or congregation or in other interpersonal settings – can we appropriate and internalise our call to be in trinitarian relatedness. In that context we gradually realise that our trinitarian God is to be encountered not in another world, but in the New Reign at the heart of this world, proclaimed and inaugurated (from a Christian viewpoint) in the life and mission of Jesus.

CHAPTER FIVE

The feminine frame:
Reclaiming a subverted tradition

The task for feminists now is the con-questioning con-questing for the deep sources of the questions seeking a permanent altering state of consciousness.

Mary Daly

In Christian religious life today women outnumber men by three to one. Yet practically all the laws governing the vowed life are drawn up by men, and are based upon masculine values of rationality, exclusion, heroism and control. Most women religious still work in apostolates where the masculine urge to dominate and achieve prevails. In both male and female forms the feminine qualities of feeling, imagination, creativity, inclusion, the freedom to unfold and a passion for justice are largely subverted.

Once again we are witnessing an unbalanced and distorted treatment of ancient historical roots. Contemporary writers – some of whom do not favour the distinction between feminine and masculine values – equate the depreciation of the feminine with the rise of classical science in the fifteenth century. With the *machine* as the dominant metaphor, everything was construed to function in mechanistic fashion, with the masculine cerebral manipulator firmly and clearly in control. This linear mode of perception and understanding could neither entertain nor tolerate the lateral requirements of imagination and intuition. There is little room for the artist in a highly technological culture.

Pre-patriarchal value radiation

But the Industrial Revolution, the progeny of classical science, is merely the culmination of a dominant patriarchal orientation dating back almost 10,000 years to the dawn of the Agricultural Revolution. Even that expanded frame of reference is inadequate to highlight the centrality and impact of the feminine in human and planetary culture. No epoch illustrates this more cogently and convincingly than that of the great goddess worshipped throughout the palaeolithic era as far back as 40,000 BCE and prevailing well into the last millennium of pre-Christian times. (More on this topic in Stone 1976; Eisler 1987; Sjoo and Mor 1987).

The contention that patriarchy was preceded by a long phase of matriarchy is not immediately relevant to our considerations and therefore will not be explored. What are of concern are those deep archetypal values that surface in liminal experience, of which those described as feminine are of central importance. I refer particularly to that aggregate of *relational* experiences:

- that can hold together in a creative synthesis the opposites that the masculine consciousness tends to construe in a divisively dualistic way;
- that can enhance a sense of freedom and flow in all life's processes which the masculine mode seeks to 'conquer and control';
- that cherishes the wild, passionate, erotic instincts that underpin creativity and justice which the masculine seeks to subvert, label and repress;
- that seeks to participate in the evolving process of life, rather than control it through hierarchical and patriarchal domination.

These are the deep archetypal values of which contemporary culture is seriously deprived. And the human heart will remain largely unfulfilled until we reconnect with those primal qualities which belong to our deep collective psyche. Even throughout the patriarchal era (from 8,000 BCE onwards) the feminine power (usually, but not exclusively, embodied in woman) keeps surfacing. Thus we have an extensive worship of the goddess dominating the first 4,000 years of the Agricultural Revolution, remnants of which continue in tribal religions to the present time (see the comprehensive review in Eisler 1987). We know of shamannesses as well as shamans; and prophetesses as well as prophets (the literature consistently gives priority to the male forms). We know that in ancient Hinduism and in early Buddhism female monastics also flourished, as they do to this day (see Tsomo 1988). In the early Christian Church, virgins feature earlier, and in greater numbers, than the male monastics. And for practically the entire Christian era females have contributed to the growth and expansion of the vowed life at least as much as males – often exceeding them in every respect.

Religious life, in its popular historical depiction, presents not merely a misleading picture, but one that is grossly distorted and unjust. Most of the historical records were compiled by men, themselves schooled almost exclusively in a dominant male culture. By addressing a feminine frame of reference we are attempting to retrieve and reclaim one of the oldest, richest and culturally significant strands of liminal experience. Without this dimension our attempts at reframing religious life will remain seriously deficient.

In most Christian circles, reference to the goddess smacks of paganism and the primitive beliefs of pre-civilisation. Such perceptions tend to be uninformed, often biased and reactionary. Even Christians who strive to be open to such insights are often spiritually and intellectually restricted, because neither their education nor formation has included such considerations. To this day our religious and spiritual culture is heavily masculine, and consequently devoid of breadth and depth.

Retrieving long-lost values

Today anthropologists and ethnographers date human spiritual development to *c.* 70,000 BCE, when burial customs reveal a distinctive spiritual awareness. It is another 30,000 years, however, before we encounter an inculturation of the spiritual that exhibits succinct and highly complex customs and mores, with the female god as a central motif. Much of our evidence for this claim comes from Ice Age art which some scholars date as early as 40,000 BCE, peaking around 25,000 BCE and beginning to diminish with the emergence of the Agricultural Revolution around 8,000 BCE.

There is a great deal of evidence for goddess worship in the upper palaeolithic era (40,000-10,000 BCE). A vast range of sculptured images and cave paintings have been identified and although open to different interpretations, it is noteworthy that female figurines (often called 'venuses') outnumber male ones by ten to one. The dominant themes of fertility, menstruation, copulation, pregnancy, birth and lactation are also unmistakably female. The religious/spiritual significance of these figures, although long debated among scholars, is now widely accepted.

To the modern viewer these ancient images are easily dismissed as crude, primitive and unenlightened. Many consist of grotesquely large and obese drawings, possibly suggesting an image of woman as prodigiously fertile and full of life. Falk (1987, pp. 303-304) suggests that the enlarged forms and the frequent depictions of the female torso without head, hands or feet are artistic devices to illustrate the close identity of woman, and especially female fertility, with the body of the Earth itself.

It is the predominance of fertility symbolism that erroneously leads many scholars to link goddess-worship with the neolithic era (10,000-4,000 BCE) and the rise of agriculture as a dominant way of life. The archaeological discoveries of Catal Huyuk (in southern Turkey), excavated by James Mellaart in 1961-1963, while confirming features of an earlier tradition, also indicate a distinctive shift away from the female as the central embodiment of spiritual values. As the male will to power and control gradually came to the fore throughout the neolithic era we lost sight of the deeper archetypal significance of the palaeolithic goddess-worship.

Ice Age art was first discovered about 150 years ago and is now largely associated with centres such as the Dordogne region of southern France (especially Lascaux) Vogelherd (west Germany) Altamira (northern Spain), Willendorf, in (Austria) and Mezin (Ukraine); it is now generally accepted that rockshelter paintings discovered in Australia, Tasmania, Tanzania and South Africa belong to the same genre (Leakey 1992 pp. 314 ff). Several interpretations have been offered, ranging from sympathetic magic focused on the hunt (hence the animal figures), to idol worship of various types, to infantile and primitive projections born out of fear and ignorance. Today most interpreters (of whom Margaret Conkey of the University of California at Berkeley is a leading authority) adopt an open and receptive attitude, tacitly (and often openly) acknowledging the complex and profound motifs that are being depicted and explored. One of the better known scholars, Leroi-Gourhan (1968), suggests that an appreciation of ancient mythology is essential to a proper interpretation, which may then produce something akin to a cosmological synthesis, manifesting a highly developed wholistic, intuitive and spiritual consciousness.

The goddess and archetypal values

There is a deep archetypal significance to the culture of goddess worship, embodying and articulating values which contemporary liminal groups will seek to reclaim consciously or unconsciously (the latter for the greater part). These include:

a. *The power of the feminine for passionate creativity.*
Today most scholars following Bruns (1973 pp. 9-10),
agree that it was women and not men who actually pro-
duced these ancient drawings. When the feminine spirit is
set free creativity overflows. A more free and open-ended
dynamic ensues between people themselves, between humans and other life-forms, between creatures and creation
(the planet). The interdependence and interrelatedness of
all things becomes the normative mode for value-commu-
nication and mutual interaction.

We are presented with a very different image of society
from the one we currently know. It is equalitarian (see
Eisler 1987 p. 206 n. 10), flexible, unstructured, relying
more on creative process than on formal political or ecclesiastical structures. To the modern reader it sounds danger-
ously close to anarchy and outright chaos. But this is a
projection from the present to the past, one that conveniently circumvents the overload of anarchy and chaos that
prevails in our so-called civilized world.

b. *The inculturation of the spiritual as a central unify-
ing value.* In palaeolithic art, as in most other aspects of
that culture, the currently destructive (masculine) dualism
between the sacred and the secular was unknown. It was
the essential *unity* of all things that mattered, the deep
intuitive realisation that the creative energy (what today we
call God) was within the unfolding process and not external to it. In this primordial vision we have all the ingredi-
ents of the new cosmology (see Swimme and Berry 1992;
Sahtouris 1989; Lovelock 1979; 1988); little wonder it
speaks so deeply to our hearts and imaginations.

When we internalise a sense of our planet as *one* (and
the cosmos also) we readily appreciate the interdependence of all life-forms. Initially one may be surprised by
the abundance of animal depictions in Ice Age art. They
seem to be portrayed as being as important as human
beings. (Strangely, fishes and birds only feature in a
minimal way.) There is no clear-cut interpretation of what

the animals signify, but their close interrelationship with humans and the probable religious significance of this liaison are dimensions that most scholars acknowledge. Important implications begin to emerge for a fresh understanding of our vow of stewardship; these will be explored in chapter six.

c. *Reclaiming our identity as embodied persons*. The literature on the Great Mother Goddess tends to describe her divine power in corporeal and earthly terms. Contrary to the many derogatory descriptions in the monotheistic religions, the Goddess is unambiguously an embodied presence, whose bodily processess, especially her fertility and sexuality, are unashamedly cherished and affirmed. Of particular interest is the ancient understanding that the body of the Goddess is also the earth's own body. Embodiment and earthiness assume spiritual, and even theological, significance. In the wholistic vision of those ancient times, embodiment is not a 'source of temptation' but the very element that connects us most powerfully to the power of the divine itself.

In our own time, women struggle to reclaim the long suppressed story of their identity as embodied persons (see the comprehensive analysis of Raphael 1996). But this is not merely a female issue. Men, too, have been disembodied by the culture of mechanisation which views all creatures as objects to be controlled and conquered (Cf., Lawlor 1989: Nelson & Longfellow 1994). Motivated by the rediscovery of these ancient and profound values, women lead the way in trying to reclaim the embodied nature of all reality – the ultimate basis for a truly incarnational worldview.

d. *The central importance of fertility* could easily denote an underlying fear of extinction in a culture where we assume that survival was an ongoing struggle. This is just one of several misleading assumptions we frequently make. For much of the era under consideration people lived with relative abundance rather than in a state of deprivation. We are dealing with the era of *Homo sapiens sapiens* by which time humans had become quite adept at the skills of survival. Moreover, climatic conditions for much of this time were favourable to the flourishing of plant, animal and human life.

The fertility cult, therefore, may be more a celebration of life than a magical or religious attempt to deflect impending disaster. The voluminous figurines illustrate a culture of abundance, relishing and quite unashamedly rejoicing in its proclivity. The central religious image was that of *woman giving birth*, and not, as in our time, the often necrophilic symbol of a *man dying on a cross*; love of life, rather than fear of death, prevailed in this ancient culture. Here we encounter no alienation from the surrounding world; the modern theological notion of *co-creativity* seems to have been the central norm.

   e. *Sexuality as a sacred power to be cherished and celebrated.* From within that bond with creation and the vocation to co-create comes a sense of sexuality largely devoid of the hang-ups and deviations of our contemporary culture. There is an undeniable sense of the goodness of the human body, the sensuousness of the flesh, the intimacy and closeness of human bonding (and a close affiliation with other life-forms), the erotic delight in the pleasures and joys of life. And fortunately it appears that there were no moralists around to set people on guilt trips.

Within this primal tradition are many of the archetypal values of the vow for relatedness. When we strive to set aright our relationships with life-forms, including Planet Earth itself, then a more inclusive and nurturing sense of sexuality ensues. As Evola (1983) points out, long before the current preoccupation with sex as a 'mechanism' for procreation there existed a psychosexual paradigm stretching back over the millennia where the procreative function is perceived to be quite secondary and *creativity* (at every level) is the goal and purpose of all sexual relatedness.

The liminal challenge in this area is quite daunting, lumbered as we are with so much repression from patriarchal interference. This subject is comprehensively reviewed in Eisler (1995).

   f. *Reclaiming the androgynous archetype.* Bruns (1973 pp. 12-13) postulates that the bulls frequently depicted in these ancient drawings represent the male side of God suggesting a bipolar understanding of God but also attributing to the divine an *androgynous* nature. This is yet another topic of archetypal significance which invokes a fresh response in our time. Both Singer (1977) and Fiand (1987) invite a reappraisal of the androgynous archetype, a reality often depicted as the ultimate sexual aberration, characterised by deviancy and confusion. Archetypally, the androgyne is always presented as divinely endowed, and is often portrayed as a symbolic restoration of 'chaos', the undifferentiated union that preceded the Creation. It also symbolises that state in which the erotic no longer has to be sought or pursued, because it is always present in its totality.

   Most formal religions focus on the splitting of the androgyne whereas pre-religious culture is mainly concerned with the fusion of its opposite poles. The tendency towards divisive dualisms is once more apparent. And throughout the epoch of formal religion a recurring theme is that of attributing androgynous identity to great founders like Jesus (Berdyaev, Koepgen, Eliade, Jung) and the Buddha not to mention the several androgynous divinities that Hinduism acknowledges to this day.

   It seems to me that the celibate vocation cannot be fully understood or internalized without acknowledging and integrating the androgynous dimension, and the Matthean reference to those who make themselves eunuchs for the sake of God's New Reign (Matt 19:12) may need to be reinterpreted against this background. The liminal celibate – and in all forms of liminality there are echoes of the celibate archetype – is called to embrace and hold on behalf of humanity something of that primal human-divine

THE FEMININE FRAME

To illustrate this strand, I use a diagram of the human energy field, focussed on the seven chakras, the central energy points from which all the meridians flow. Working upward from the base, we note the following key elements explored in this chapter.

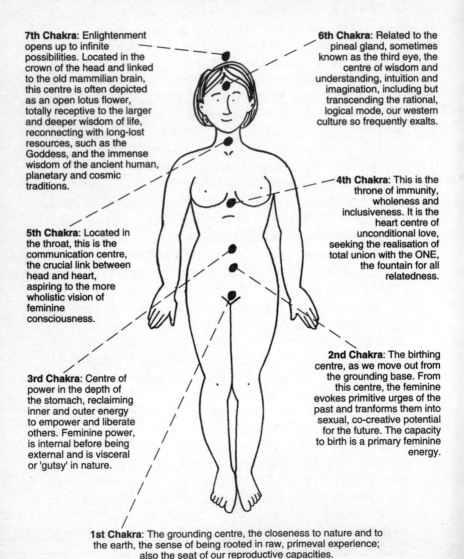

7th Chakra: Enlightenment opens up to infinite possibilities. Located in the crown of the head and linked to the old mammilian brain, this centre is often depicted as an open lotus flower, totally receptive to the larger and deeper wisdom of life, reconnecting with long-lost resources, such as the Goddess, and the immense wisdom of the ancient human, planetary and cosmic traditions.

6th Chakra: Related to the pineal gland, sometimes known as the third eye, the centre of wisdom and understanding, intuition and imagination, including but transcending the rational, logical mode, our western culture so frequently exalts.

5th Chakra: Located in the throat, this is the communication centre, the crucial link between head and heart, aspiring to the more wholistic vision of feminine consciousness.

4th Chakra: This is the throne of immunity, wholeness and inclusiveness. It is the heart centre of unconditional love, seeking the realisation of total union with the ONE, the fountain for all relatedness.

3rd Chakra: Centre of power in the depth of the stomach, reclaiming inner and outer energy to empower and liberate others. Feminine power, is internal before being external and is visceral or 'gutsy' in nature.

2nd Chakra: The birthing centre, as we move out from the grounding base. From this centre, the feminine evokes primitive urges of the past and tranforms them into sexual, co-creative potential for the future. The capacity to birth is a primary feminine energy.

1st Chakra: The grounding centre, the closeness to nature and to the earth, the sense of being rooted in raw, primeval experience; also the seat of our reproductive capacities.

yearning for wholeness, completion and the realignment of our 'divided' selves. Whether or not this total union is achievable (either here or in eternity) is not our concern; it is the *yearning* itself and all it awakens in us in our desire for harmony and reconciliation – at a range of different levels in the human-planetary unfolding – that is of liminal significance.

g. Although impossible to define or describe, a distinctive sense of *community* prevailed in this ancient goddess culture. Sieveking (1983 p. 5) notes that many drawings depict *groups* of figurines, rather than single ones. Cultic and ritual reasons are readily offered, but there may be a communal motif of much deeper significance, highlighting once more the feminine capacity to inter-relate in a co-operative, non-competitive, non-hierarchical mode. The archetypal values underpinning this communitarian sense are precisely those we seek to incarnate today in our fresh understanding of the vow for partnership.

The goddess tradition embodies and illustrates in sharp relief many of those archetypal values which evoke the need for liminal people, and which demand a radical reassessment of the vowed life, particularly the meaning and significance of the vows themselves.

h. Finally there is the imaging of God as woman, with related metaphorical and theological implications. Johnson (1994) argues that our adopted values (she is referring specifically to Religious) always relate to specific modes of imaging and experiencing God. The mother-woman image denotes a nurturing sustaining passionate, protective and participative God, very different from the distant, patriarchal, judgmental God we frequently encounter in mainstream religion and in much of modern evangelism. Religious life makes no sense apart from a belief in God, but the God-image out of which we live and witness often impedes, rather than liberates, the liminal and prophetic edge of our mission and lifestyle.

Throughout the period of patriarchal supremacy, women and feminine values were gradually eroded. With the rise of formal religions, beginning with Hinduism about 2,500 BCE, the feminine is not merely diminished but deemed to be deviant, dangerous, a source of temptation. All the world religions carry a strong anti-feminine bias, a tendency to depreciate and even undermine its power. Currently Islam is the most sexist of the major faiths.

The contribution of Christian female religious

In the formal religious traditions, female religious have never been allowed to tell their unique story. Developments in the female vowed life – numerically, culturally and ministerially – have been every bit as outstanding as the male versions (see McNamara 1996), but have been completely overshadowed by the latter. In many cases, no attempt was made to record or preserve what the women were about. And the few references we have tend to follow a stereotyped version, rendering the female or feminine story in terms of the male culture or the prevailing masculine value system.[8]

A cursory glance at the story of female Christian religious life will illustrate this historical cultural and spiritual imbalance. Preceding any formal male developments were the *virgins*, formally recognized by the Church and existing possibly as early as 100 CE. Apparently they lived in their own homes, and congregated for communal prayer and charitable service. Many of the early Church fathers allude to the creative, courageous and exemplary life and service of the virgins whose consecration did not segregate them from the world, but put them more deeply in touch with it.[9]

Next we note that many of the outstanding founders from Anthony of Egypt right through to Francis in the thirteenth century had mothers, sisters, or close female relatives in the religious life. In the West, our first evidence for the existence of female communities is that of St Augustine, who, during his episcopate at Hippo, addressed a treatise to the Virgins of the city. The nature of religious consecration at this time was determined according to the rubrics of each local church. Our first evidence for a more universal formula comes from the Gelasian Sacramentary of the sixth century.

From the seventh to the tenth centuries some foundresses and abbesses assumed powers usually reserved to bishops, abbots and the ordained clergy. Many of these communities consisted of double monasteries, with male and female groups living adjacently. Women often ruled these communities. As abbess, such a woman exercised both religious and secular power. Because of the lands held in the name of the Order, she was responsible for fulfilling the feudal obligations of a vassal and for the administration of the manors and fields upon which the maintenance of the community depended. She also catered for the spiritual needs of those living on the monastery lands, the collection of tithes and the choice of the village clergy. In exercising these powers women acted on a par with their male counterparts.

Literacy in these early centuries meant the ability to read Latin, a skill often reserved to bishops, monks and clergy. From the seventh century on we learn of abbesses introducing opportunities for women to learn Latin: e.g., Repton in Derbyshire, England (where Aelfthrith was abbess); Chelles in France; Quedlinberg and Gandersheim in Germany. Thus equipped, such women assumed other ecclesiastical and political responsibilities. In the mid seventh century, Salaberga of Laon in France founded seven churches and took responsibility for 300 nuns. Her contemporary St Fara founded a joint community at Brie in the north of France, ruled as abbess, and assumed priestly and episcopal power, hearing confessions and excommunicating members. In the twelfth century at the Spanish abbey of Las Huelgas the nuns appointed their own confessors. As late as 1230 the abbess Dona Sanchia Garcia blessed the novices like a priest and presided at chapter meetings for the twelve other monasteries under her authority.

Among the outstanding monastic women of this epoch was Hrotsvit of Gandersheim (*c.* 930-990), poet, historian and the only person to write drama in Europe between the fourth and eleventh centuries. Harrad of Landsberg abbess of Hohenberg in Alsace (1167-1195), founded a community of canons, a community of nuns and a hospital, while excelling in a thorough knowledge of the Church Fathers and other classical authors. Of all these abbesses, perhaps the best known is Hildegard of Bingen (1098-1179), whose scientific treatises impressed both popes and emperors. She was also a doctor, pharmacist, playwright, poet, painter and musician.

But already, in the twelfth century, attempts were under way to halt the upsurge of feminine and womanly power. The orders of Fontevrault in France (*c.* 1100) and Sempringham in England (*c.* 1150) were founded with a small quota of priests to act as chaplains, administrators and confessors to the nuns. The canonical *Decretum* (*c.* 1140) confirmed that only males could be ordained, and subsequently, ecclesiastical learning became the initiative and reserve of clerics. In 1215 the Fourth Lateran Council decreed that all future foundations in religious life should follow the Rule of St Benedict for contemplatives, and that of St Augustine for apostolic groups. The final blow to women was the Bull *Periculoso* of Pope Boniface VIII in 1298, which stated that nuns were neither to leave their cloisters nor receive outsiders. In fact it was only after the Council of Trent (1545-1563) that enclosure was enforced with full impact.

Beyond the restrictions of enclosure

Meanwhile, the feminine spirit, ever imaginative and inventive, and, it seems, never to be completely outdone, shifts the creative energy elsewhere: *underground*, in the eyes of the official Church; into the heart of the world in the eyes of those to whom it really mattered. Throughout the eleventh and twelfth centuries a range of alternative women's groups emerged, seeking to follow the monastic ideal at the heart of the world. Foremost among these were the Beguines, who earned widespread following and support in France, Belgium and west Germany. Although at times critical of the official Church, they kept close links, especially through the Franciscans and Dominicans. One of their better known members, Mechtild of Magdeburg (1210-1280), lived her final years as a Dominican nun.

Other alternative groups of the time included the Beghards (open to men and women), who denounced the Church's desire to legislate and control every dimension of faith experience, and advocated an alternative 'free spirit', devoid of legal or sacramental links with the Church. The Lollards in England, the Guglielmites in Italy and the Cathari (Albigensians) in southern France followed a similar path of dissent. Because these groups were all denounced as heretical, historians (especially males) rarely allude to the alternative value system they were striving to safeguard within a Church that was becoming more and more oppressive. While not wishing to concur with their extreme ascetical practices – possibly a subconscious excessive zeal for archetypal values – their cultural, historical and feminine significance must not be underestimated. Only with such a reassessment of history can we hope to engage in a more enlightened way with the liminal movements of our own time.

The feminist consciousness of the Middle Ages impacted on men as well as on women. In terms of religious life this is nowhere more apparent than in the life and example of St Francis of Assisi, with his profound love for the poor and for nature. (Ironically, he seems to have concurred with many of the Church's derogatory attitudes towards women.) The early Cistercians also exemplified some unique feminine traits. Although Southern (1970 p. 314) claims that no religious body was more thoroughly masculine in its temperament and discipline than the Cistercians '...none that shunned female contact with greater determination or that raised more formidable barriers against the intrusion of women', Bynum (1975) reminds us that the outstanding Cistercian writers of the twelfth century, Bernard of Clairvaux, William of St Thierry, Aelred of Rievaulx, Adam of Perseigne and Stephen of Coteaux all exhibit a literary style different from that of previous and subsequent centuries. '[They] make frequent reference to emotion [especially love]... show an awareness of relationships among equals... and see interpersonal relationships as an incentive to compassion and a setting for learning humility' (Bynum p. 276).

This apparent contradiction is worthy of comment. Historical fact as overtly observed can reveal a set of behaviours and values that may seem quite sexist. When we connect with the myth (story), as revealed through writing or other symbolic mediation, we begin to see something quite different. Tragically, the external forces can be so imposing and culturally validated that they all but destroy the deeper archetypal values seeking expression. What happens in time is that the liminal focus shifts to another cultural setting; the original locale will then lose its cultural significance, may become a self-perpetuating ideology (which could last for centuries) and will eventually die out.

It is this shift in liminal focus that launches a new image of women in the religious life of the fifteenth, sixteenth and seventeenth centuries. Enclosure was the norm for all vowed women; yet the limited records from the plague-ridden Europe of the late fourteenth century (the Black Death) suggest outstanding care and hospitality by the 'enclosed' nuns. This may well have been the springboard for a new strand of feminine and female witness for which Angela Merici (1474-1540), foundress of the Ursulines, is a prototypical figure.

Angela herself never became a Religious remaining a

94

Franciscan tertiary until she died. In order to be as fully as possible at the service of the sick, the poor, the elderly and marginalised Angela instructed her Sisters to live in their own homes, retaining their *lay* identity. They met in small groups to pray and support each other in their works of charity. Angela died in 1540, merely five years after having founded the Ursulines; her final words include a plea to her Sisters to retain adaptability as a key virtue for the future.

Charles Borromeo nurtured the orphaned group through many tensions and struggles, eventually winning papal approbation for a *conventual*, but not a cloistered, existence. Thus there was set a precedent that in subsequent centuries would only be preserved against great odds. Despite the unique and outstanding contribution of women religious, or maybe precisely because of it there continue to this day unrelenting efforts to couch and structure the female contribution according to the whims and wishes of our predominately male clerical Church.

Probably the next outstanding names in the gradual liberalisation and affirmation of the female contribution are that of Vincent de Paul (1580-1660) and his co-foundress of the Daughters of Charity, Louise de Marillac. Vincent's vision for the new group is often cited: 'They are to have no monastery but the houses of the sick, who have for cells only a lodging or the poorest room, whose chapel is the parish Church who have the streets for cloisters. They are enclosed only by obedience; they make the fear of God their "grille" and they have no veil but their own modesty'.

Contemporaneous with Vincent de Paul was a woman of prophetic stature, Mary Ward (1585-1645) foundress of the Institute of the Blessed Virgin Mary. She had received the inspiration to found an apostolic institute for women with a centralized government, like those already formed by men's institutes. The English clergy felt threatened, reacted negatively and denounced her publicly. The controversy was carried to Rome where Mary valiantly defended her cause but in vain: her Congregation was suppressed by Pope Urban VIII in 1631. She was forced into exile in Munich, eventually returning to England, where she died without seeing her dream come to fruition. Time would vindicate her aspirations. Eventually her Congregation was granted papal approbation in 1877 and today it flourishes in 20 countries across the world.

A timely example in the same vein is that of Mary MacKillop (1842-1909), foundress of the Sisters of St Joseph in Australia, beatified in January 1995. Mary was a tenacious woman who let nothing stand in the way of her unrelenting care for the poor and underprivileged. In that process she was forced to endure a great deal of slander and ridicule at the hands of bishops and clergy culminating in her excommunication by the Bishop of Adelaide in 1871 (lifted the next year, just before the bishop died) and her eventual expulsion from the diocese in 1883. Time was to vindicate both the woman and her vision, and today her Sisters comprise the largest female group in Australia, contributing to people's welfare with the generous and caring spirit of their great foundress.

People such as Angela Merici, Louise de Marillac, Mary Ward and Mary MacKillop represent one of the most painful and courageous phases of male-female engagement in the history of religious life. The Council of Trent set up the *male cleric* as the supreme embodiment of the loyal faithful Catholic. Everything and everybody had to conform to this model, not of Catholic priesthood but of Catholic clericalism. Women, more than anybody else were degraded, undervalued, virtually ignored within this conformist, defensive, frightened Church. Were it not for the occasional upsurge of prophetic figures like Mary Ward, the power of the feminine would have been seriously undermined.

In the post-Tridentine era female congregations flourished. Many of their leaders and founding people battled long and hard with clerics, bishops, or with Rome itself, to safeguard their feminine and womanly uniqueness, and place it in a more creative mode at the service of God's people. Clerical interference and manipulation became widespread in a desperate attempt to control what is essentially uncontrollable. The trend continues to this day provoking serious consideration of *non-canonical status* as possibly the only honourable way to live the female vowed life in the contemporary world (an option adopted by a number of female groups in the USA in recent decades).

Contemporary developments

Currently, two starkly contrasting images of woman in religious life prevail. One is that of the loyal, unassuming hard-working woman, giving all she has to God and to people. This tends to be the type of religious sister that African Bishops seek when they establish diocesan Congregations (as many have done in recent years); recently I heard a native African sister describe it as a system of 'sisters in bondage'. The underlying philosophy is one of traditional patriarchal subservience, the immorality and degradation of which is overshadowed by the outstanding and at times heroic works of charity and mercy undertaken by these women. Undoubtedly Mother Teresa of Calcutta serves as a supreme emblem of this category of vowed woman.

The other dominant type far less numerous than the former but exerting quite a powerful influence in the world and Church of our time, is that of the Sister who cherishes the primacy of her womanhood and the uniqueness of her feminine giftedness. She fiercely and vociferously defends that uniqueness, not for the sake of protecting it, but because she believes in her heart that it is every bit as divinely-endowed and as culturally essential to our world as traditional patriarchal values have been in the past. Such conviction is quickly labelled as 'extreme feminism', which excuses those who label from having to acknowledge the profoundly grave and urgent issues that are being addressed by these women of our time, reconnecting with their deep intuitive hearts, espousing the world in a global embrace over against the masculine urge to divide and conquer, and vociferous in their rage for justice against the cumulative oppression of centuries past.

Women will continue to dominate religious life throughout the twenty-first century, and the polarisation (of the two modes outlined above) is likely to become much more pronounced. At this time of decline and disintegration in religious life, many orders and congregations are accepting candidates the genuineness of whose vocation is quite suspect. Bolstering up numbers has become something of a preoccupation and often we tend to accept candidates who are seeking security from the turbulent changing world of our time. But religious life is not about security and never should be. Liminality is predominantly about risk and not about security.

These remarks apply to men as well as to women. Their relevance for the latter is that the more traditional, subservient forms of female religious life will prevail longer than we might like to think. Consequently, those adopting a more feminine-based approach will continue to battle for formal recognition, and will often encounter stubborn resistance from a Church firmly rooted in, and desperately seeking to defend, its traditional patriarchal mode. One presumes and hopes that truth will prevail in the end and undoubtedly the Spirit will breath new life where s(he) detects it has the greatest chance of flowering for the upbuilding of God's New Reign.

Religious life is emerging from a protracted era of masculine framing. We are not suggesting a feminine reframing simply to balance things out. We are dealing with that same quantum leap impinging upon our world today at a range of different levels. The very foundations as we have known them not just for the past 400 years (Industrial Revolution), but for the past 10,000 years (Agricultural Revolution), are shifting. That primal creative and exuberant energy that animated goddess worship, and has invigorated human and planetary culture for so many millennia, is once more being ignited from its smouldering cinders. The woman who runs with the wolves (Estes 1992), that ancient archetype of wild, passionate creativity, reclaims her rightful place, jolting and even demolishing sacred rules and long-established institutions. The consequences for the vowed life are daunting and disturbing; but the fresh hope and vitality are of a quality that we have not had for a long time. Beyond the perilous transition is a bright and promising future yearning to be born afresh.

CHAPTER SIX

The pastoral frame:
Mediating relational values

*Questions will more likely lead to deeper questions
as intellect yields precedence to heart and we in our
thinking leave room for the existential and experiential; for the mystical, the paradoxical... what we
vow is open-ended, a process not a final product.*

Barbara Fiand

Religious life is associated with two dominant images: charitable service and contemplation. The former refers to those works of compassion and care focusing specifically on the poor and sick, often the utterly neglected of society. Most contemporary apostolates, although now highly formalised, bureaucratised and often focused on the rich and powerful originated in areas of acute need. Engagement of religious (sisters particularly) in parish ministry and social work, developments of more recent times, does not convey to the general public anything of the uniqueness of the vowed life; whether the social worker is a sister or a lay woman matters little.

Religious themselves tend to emphasise and prioritize the collective/corporate witness, and they perceive this as being more potent and relevant than a series of individual members doing the same work or a range of individual ministries. In male congregations, particularly, strenuous efforts are made to maintain and prioritize corporate commitments over and above individual ministries. There is no convincing evidence to suggest that the former is more effective or life-giving, either for the recipients or for the religious themselves.

In not a few cases the argument for corporate witness is

fuelled more by fear than by apostolic zeal. Today, in the West particularly, there is a widespread fear of fragmentation, and the ultimate disintegration of the order or congregation. It is often validated by a highly questionable and superficial perception (especially in the USA) that women's congregations are disintegrating because so many female religious live and work singly. From a viewpoint of pastoral witness many of these women make enormous contributions to Church and world. Moreover, many of their congregations (not necessarily all the members) cherish and formally mission them into that specific mode of life and mission.

The second dominant perception of religious is that of them being people of prayer, whose lives are dedicated to God in an exclusive way; the contemplative orders are deemed to embody this ideal with greater clarity and conviction. One wonders how widely this view is held! Is it predominately a perception of religious themselves, of clergy and some spiritually informed lay people? Rarely, it seems to me, have Christians identified with the vowed life as Buddhists tend to do. And the enclosed nature of the so-called contemplative orders smacks of a dualistic, otherworldly spirituality, which alienates, rather than empowers, today's spiritual seeker. The notion that the monastery can be a powerhouse of prayer for the world betrays a dangerous cultural projection for a world that need not take spiritual values too seriously because the monastery is doing so on its behalf.

Throughout this work I propose that religious life in its quintessential nature is about engagement with the world and not a form of opposition to it. As a counter-cultural movement, the vowed life becomes most meaningful and effective at those nerve-points where the struggle for *meaningful relationships* takes place. We live in an interdependent, interrelated world where mutual interaction is the desired mode of operating. Rarely does the interaction take place in full justice, equality and due appropriation of the diversity of giftedness that is ours as a human, planetary and cosmic species. It is in negotiating the norms, procedures and structures that facilitate the right relationships that we religious have a unique contribution to make. And that uniqueness we name our liminal prophetic calling.

Because the pastoral landscape is that of interrelatedness, then the quality and quantity of our capacity to relate assumes central importance. There is no room in religious life for the person who seeks to escape the intimacy of sex, the affective challenge of monogamous relationships or the mutuality of close friendships. A cold, distant, ascetic religious woman or man is an enigma to the witness potential of the vowed life. A warm and caring disposition is essential; so also a sense of being at ease with people, especially in their trauma and pain and in their exuberance and ecstasy. Perhaps the most needed quality is that of openness and receptivity to the changing fortunes of one's own life and that of others, with the flexibility to adopt and adjust to changing situations.

The contemporary sense of relatedness is not merely interpersonal, but also planetary and cosmic in its multidimensional nature. How we relate with the universe as we experience it in our interaction with planet earth, is not just an issue of *secular* concern. It has profound spiritual implications for many people today. Increasingly, we are realising that a just and loving relationship with God is impossible apart from the God who creates and sustains our world, with whom we are invited to be co-creators.

Because our traditional spiritual formation has been anti-world and deeply rooted in dualistic oppositional modes of relating (which in fact is the very opposite of relating) we have to unlearn our destructive attitudes and values before we can hope to assume and internalise the gospel values appropriate to the formulation and development of right relationships. That relearning process is a major aspect of the reframing being explored in the present chapter.

Community as a pastoral issue

The development of right relationships commences with the maturation of early childhood, the quality of which largely depends on the surrounding parental and familial influences. As the child matures, other influences – friends, peers, education, media, environment – will impact upon its capacity to relate. Throughout adolescence and young adulthood, people need forums to articulate and explore their feelings and perceptions around relational issues. This need becomes more pronounced in later years, confronted as we are by the complex demands and expectations of the contemporary world. Provision for the negotiation of these needs (personal, interpersonal, developmental and spiritual) is a significantly liminal challenge of our time and raises urgent questions on what it means to belong to a caring community in the context of our emerging culture.

Community denotes acceptance, mutuality, friendship and camaraderie. At a deeper level it involves growth and challenge. Where true community happens, we engage with something even more profound: spiritual growth and discernment. The deeper layer needs the more mundane one as a point of entry, and the cultivation of acceptance and befriending are key qualities for all stages. Creating this community consciousness is an urgent pastoral need of our time, one in which religious are invited to participate in a mediating and creative role.

Community is about the desire to connect and to be connected – to the well-springs of love and wisdom at the different levels of life. The human need to relate leads most of us towards close friendships and monogamous relationships, through which we can mediate our need for emotional and sexual intimacy. Even when those needs are met in a satisfactory and fulfilling way, many people yearn for a wider (and deeper) mode of interrelating. We join clubs and organisations of various types, consciously for relaxation and fun, but often affiliations forged through these outlets take on an enduring quality that may last for a whole lifetime.

When a group of people discovers a common heart (and this happens at a subconscious level long before it becomes conscious, which in fact may never happen) members feel bonded and supported in a way that not even a monogamous relationship can make possible. It is a different type of experience, apparently happening on another level. The differentiating factor, I suggest is *spiritual* in nature, although individual members may never experience it in that way. It is as if the group energy takes over the scattered unrealised aspirations of the constituent members and transports these yearnings on to a more engaging and coherent level. This process defies rational explanation but is a fairly familiar process to those acquainted with systems theory and the philosophy underpinning it.[10] When true community begins to happen, some or all individual members will realise that a type of transformative process is under way, which nobody may be quite able to make sense of; but at least some will grasp intuitively that it is a pearl of great worth awaiting further engagement and growth.

Consequently, community is not something we can easily create. It happens when the conditions are right. These include dispositions of openness, receptivity, a desire to relate authentically, and some acknowledgement that a power greater than ourselves can act among us and between us in a way that, left to our own devices, we cannot make possible. At depth, every true relationship includes not merely one but many 'unknowns'. Such is the mystery and paradox of all attempts to relate authentically.

From a pastoral and ministerial perspective, religious fare poorly when it comes to community building. Although most Constitutions devote whole sections to it, and present it as a primary ideal, in practice our functional selves, rather than our relational selves take priority. Most congregations structure their lifestyle not around the values of *being*, but those of *doing*. In many cases community signifies the way we are together for the sake of one or more ministries.

And in ministry itself the formation and building of community rarely takes precedence for religious women or men. We tend to operate the patriarchal value system of *achievement* and the *attainment of results*. We are likely to rate more highly the quantity of togetherness, rather than its quality. Many of our traditional apostolates, especially in education, reproduce the values of competition and achievement which are fundamentally alienating to the creation of true community. At a pastoral level it is an issue awaiting serious redress, both within and outside our orders and congregations.

Engaging communally with each other, and with those we accompany in mission, raises some quite original and acute questions on how we live the vows. Already I have suggested a renaming of the vows: *for* rather than *of*, and replacing *celibacy* with *relatedness*, *poverty* with *stewardship* and *obedience* with *partnership* (not entirely different from the trinitarian model proposed by Billy 1993 pp. 33-48; 236-240). The very language we use has enormous impact on how we mediate meaning and choose to explore the challenge therein to relate in new and more authentic ways. We need to make that language more feminine and inclusive; we need to shift the focus from the ascetical, with the emphasis on separation from the world, towards the aesthetic, pointing us towards the basic goodness of life that we need to reclaim; above all else we need a language that will enable and empower us to reclaim our liminal task, to reappropriate and explore afresh the significance of the vowed life for the world of our time.

Intimacy as a liminal threshold

Taking *the capacity to relate* as a fundamental value and aspiration of our world, it seems appropriate to begin with the *vow for relatedness*. This is the oldest of the three

105

vows and the only one to be canonically sanctioned in the Christian tradition before the twelfth century. In all the major traditions of religious life it characterises something of the uniqueness of the vowed state. Thus, for example, members of the Sufi Tariqahs tend to be married (in accordance with Islamic expectations), but when ministering formally within or on behalf of the Order refrain totally from sexual and intimate interaction. Similarly in Japan, where many Buddhist monks marry, when on official temple duty they sever all links with spouse and family and remain sexually continent.

All these examples beget a widely accepted conclusion: sexual intimate enagagement blocks or militates against intimacy with God and one's service to people on behalf of God. This has been a dominant Christian conviction (and quite widespread in other religions too – Hinduism being a notable exception) that has been largely abrogated in recent times, and not without some disturbing consequences. Formal religions seem to have difficulty in acknowledging the divine origin and blessing of sexuality, with its joy, pleasure, productivity, healing power, and its capacity to unite people in deep love. Instead we have inherited a long convoluted religious tradition of sexual ambivalence, even hatred of sex, imbued with irrational fear and grotesque levels of repression. One has good reason to believe that this negative imaging of sexuality is a by-product of our patriarchal culture seeking to conquer and control one of nature's most beautiful, creative and volatile energies.

For many centuries, therefore, abstinence from sex was deemed to be an eminently holy and heroic achievement, validated in a powerful way by the imposition of celibacy on male clerics in the Catholic tradition. It is this latter development, which has only been reinforced universally since the Council of Trent (1545-1563), that has grossly distorted and overshadowed the meaning of celibacy in the monastic and religious life. In the eyes of the general public and in the self-understanding of some religious, we are celibate because the clergy are celibate. Indeed, it is this clerically-based modelling that has governed the spirituality and the legal norms of all three vows since the Council of Trent.

The *vow for relatedness* espoused by religious serves a *totally different* purpose from that of clerical celibacy. The latter, it seems to me, is a canonical regulation imposed to elicit a better quality of priestly service to people. The vow for *relatedness*, on the other hand, belongs to the prophetic liminal tradition, serving value-radiation and value media-tion on behalf of the wider human community. It is this latter dimension that concerns us in the present work.

In archetypal terms, the vow for *relatedness* is a call to name, explore and mediate the human engagement in inti-mate relationships, *within* the changing circumstances of life and culture. The celibate liminar, therefore, embodies and articulates the challenge and struggle to understand, negotiate and internalise the exchange of intimate love. Why does it have to be a non-married person? This is a paradox that cannot be comprehended solely on the level of the rational mind. Like all paradoxes, it embodies a truth that cannot be fully comprehended by human reason alone.

We are dealing with an archetypal value system relating to human and sexual intimacy for which the institution of marriage is widely perceived to be the most authentic mode of inculturation. But marital interaction and genital inti-macy, while special and important in their own right, are merely the manifest mediations of something much more complex and profound. The paradox under consideration points to the transcendent desire in every sexual engage-ment towards a fullness and completion that this life can never fully provide, the shadow side of which is that feel-ing of incompleteness (and guilt) which often accompanies sexual intimate interaction.

While wishing to explain as fully as possible the mean-ing of this vow (and the others also) we need to safeguard that mysterious dimension which defies all attempts at a fully rational explanation. As Balducelli (1975) indicates, the call to celibacy is not something one consciously

107

chooses; it is something that happens as part of one's response to a larger call. According to Balducelli, celibacy chooses us rather than we choosing it. The ability to acknowledge, accept and internalise this mysterious and paradoxical call is essential if the religious woman or man is to live this vow with a degree of integrity and equanimity.

If this is something of what the gift is about then what are its pastoral implications? It is in exploring these that the real nature of the vocation radiates and also that the paradox assumes almost frightening proportions – in the light of which we may begin to understand the reluctance shown by the great prophets in responding to their call.

The liminal person is called to be deeply in tune with contemporary culture and especially with its struggle to grow in harmony, beauty and wholeness. In terms of the vow for relatedness, this means engaging with the unfolding psychosexual issues that are uppermost at this time. Firstly, we need to acknowledge the changing nature of human sexuality itself, something our dominantly patriarchal culture considers to be stable, static and unchanging, despite overwhelming evidence to the contrary.

Since 1950 we have experienced two major waves of change in this area: a) from sexuality focused on procreation to one giving prior attention to the mutual intimate nourishment of the partners (normatively assumed to be a heterosexual married couple); b) from the latter to a more amorphous diffusion of sexual (and genital) expression in intimate human friendships (whether married or not, whether heterosexual or homosexual). This latter is more a development of the 1970s and 1980s, and is well articulated by Ferguson (1982) in her conviction that, increasingly, human intimacy will be mediated in a *breadth* of relationships, rather than in a depth of relatedness.

To some readers these preliminary observations will seem dangerous, deviant, even downrightly promiscuous, and totally alien to what celibacy is about. Two points need to be made to flesh out the scenario being depicted:

a. In our predominantly patriarchal culture inner and outer reality tend to be kept apart in a neat dualistic division. Many people can readily acknowledge and internalise profound change in the *outer* world; this inevitably means an equally profound change in the *inner* world even in the depths of our psychological selves. Inner and outer are fundamentally one – what affects the one affects the other.

b. When profound change of this nature is happening we are – at the subconscious level – disposed afresh to primeval and primal influences. In this case, archetypal sexual values arise in fresh relief claiming our acknowledgement and response. What we will tend to encounter are those pre-patriarchal energies when sexuality was more about the release of creativity, passion and spirituality than about human reproduction (see Evola 1983; Eisler 1995); the latter is an interpretation of human sexuality that emanated with the Industrial Revolution of the seventeenth century, one that ably matches the mechanistic consciousness of that epoch. Perhaps the reader also needs to be reminded that mon-ogamous marriage as we know it today (in the West) is very much the product of the late Middle Ages; only at the Council of Trent did Christian marriage assume sacramental status.

The current breakdown in traditional family, marital and sexual values tends to be attributed to the secularisation of contemporary western society. This perception is based on the naive assumption that those values (and their accompanying systems) of the past few hundred years have been with us since the dawn of civilisation; and some (e.g., sexuality) we assume to be fixed and unchanged from time immemorial. We also tend to make the false assumption that any attempt at reworking values from our past is automatically cascading into primitive chaos; and perhaps worst of all is the assumption that we humans are always fully in charge (or should be) of what is emerging in our rapidly changing world.

It is perceptions of this nature that liminal people are called upon to challenge and reframe. These are the ideologies of our patriarchal culture, which deviate our hearts and spirits from the true God, whose creativity far outstretches our restricted perceptions and whose greatness far outlives the congealed institutions we invent and idolise. It is the task of the prophet to paint the larger picture, criticise the functional and oppressive *status-quo*, and energise us towards new and risky futures (cf. Brueggemann 1978; 1986). In this pursuit of *wholeness* (rather than *perfection*) we go through the dark and sinister shadow; we do not try to circumvent or bypass it. The dominant fear is that the 'forces of evil' may destroy us. What we fail to realise is the more imminent destructibility of our currently approved ways of doing things; for example, the incidence of rape and the abuse of women within formal marriage far outstrips its frequency outside marriage but because it happens within the formally sanctioned structure it is rarely named and scarcely ever confronted.

For many people today, the path of psychosexual growth has become quite complex and, correspondingly, convoluted instead of enriched. The sexual maturity once thought to be achieved in late adolescence takes much longer to ensue, simply because life in general is more complex. The clear dualistic delineation between male and female has broken down; many people experience a sense of androgynous fusion and, often scared to talk about it, they suppress this potentially rich experience, thus adding to an already overload of sexual repression. Sexually, many people fluctuate between same-sex attraction and other-sex attraction often getting enmeshed in the gay, lesbian or bisexual stereotypes, thus failing to negotiate the otherwise creative upsurge taking place in their inner being. People who feel spiritually ecstatic in moments of heightened erotic arousal tend to suppress the voice of the Spirit because of guilt overload from the past or basic ignorance of the rich spiritual potential of their psychosexual experience.

At a societal level we confront even more complex

issues: gross and highly lucrative pornography (especially of the female body) satiating the human spirit with irrational sensory cravings totally devoid of feeling or meaning; rampant sexual abuse of youth in particular, much of which is performed by people who themselves were abused, often within a context which we naively assumed to have been highly moral, caring and loving. And most disturbing of all are the cultural symbols of our collective repression, nowhere more apparent than in the weaponry of war, much of which has an unmistakable phallic symbolism. In modern warfare more than anywhere else the sexually intoxicated patriarchal male acts out his fantasies for pleasure, manipulation and control.[11]

How can any human being or group of people be expected to assume the liminal and prophetic task of addressing this reality not to rectify it, but to help to change the consciousness that validates and generates it in the first place? A rather daunting task indeed but this is precisely what liminal groups are for. This is the reason why we bring them into being, to be catalysts to negotiate those deep issues that impinge powerfully upon our lives and affect us for weal or for woe. At a merely human level it is an impossible – even outrageous – undertaking, but like St Paul, we can pray with courage and faith: God's grace is sufficient for us.

Pastorally, therefore, the liminal celibate is called to explore and mediate *on behalf of the people* the deeper symbolic significance of the psychosexual agenda of today's world: to decipher its meaning and evolution, to probe its archetypal significance, to denounce those systems which seek to stymie and stultify erotic creativity, and to offer processes for negotiating its impact on human and planetary life. One is not suggesting that this task is reserved to liminal people. In fact, anybody who strives to engage with it at this level adopts something of the liminal space, but the formal liminars (which previously we have identified as the religious) are missioned in a special way for this undertaking.

And what of the pastoral care of the celibates themselves? In many religious communities around the world, sex is still a taboo subject; and the destructive force of that secrecy is nowhere more apparent than in the tendency towards paedophilia among religious, an issue which has surfaced in recent years. Many religious, in loneliness and often feeling bereft, struggle with sexual urges and desires. Many communities fail to mediate any sense of tender touch or tactile reassurance. Many celibates are starved of real human sexual love.

This often raises questions on the wisdom of the total exclusion of genital intimacy for celibates. As already indicated, this is permitted in some traditions which pastorally and spiritually may be every bit as meaningful and profound as our austere Christian approach. None the less, the tradition of total abstinence has a hallowed ring to it, and symbolically denotes a quality of complete allegiance to the commitment involved in liminal witness.

However, it needs to be openly acknowledged that some celibates in the Christian tradition avail of genital intimacy, usually for short or sporadic periods of time; some openly admit that this has deepened their sense of calling, enhanced their human growth and reinforced their love and respect for the people they minister to. That the vow for relatedness will include the possibility of genital interaction in the future is something we cannot totally exclude. This is not an attempt at compromise, nor a sell-out on idealism, but an aspiration to remain as open as possible to the changing nature of human sexuality and the manner in which it can best be integrated in the lives of those called to the vowed commitment in the years ahead.

One of the most delicate issues in this field of witness is the desirable balance between disclosure and appropriate privacy. For most people, sexuality is a very private dimension of experience; at one level this relates to its sacredness and to its uniqueness for each person. None the less, there is no such thing as a totally private sexual life, and sexual energy, of its very nature and because of its enormous erotic creative potential, inundates every aspect of our culture. All human interaction – even human and animal contact – has sexual connotations. We cannot be other than sexual people, and in one sense the more sexual we are the more authentically human we become. It is in over-privatising the sexual drive and its conscious suppression, or, worst of all, its unconscious repression, that we beget demons who reap havoc in our lives personally, interpersonally and globally. To bring sexuality out of the proverbial closet is one of the most urgent needs of our time, a process best facilitated by people who have worked long and hard to integrate the graced experience of being fully sexual themselves; this is probably the greatest single challenge confronting the sexual celibate of our time.

Stewardship for our planet

Most updated versions of religious life constitutions include one or more references to 'a preferential option for the poor'. The phrase, initially coined at the Latin American theological conference held at Pueblo in 1968, evokes feelings of guilt on the one hand and reaction on the other. Guilt, because many of us Christians know deep in our hearts that we fail dismally in espousing the cause of the poor and oppressed as the Gospels challenge us to do; reaction, because the challenge scares us and we do not much like to be disturbed out of the prevailing comfortable middle-class culture that dominates Christian religious life today.

At one level, religious warm to the notion of a preferential option for the poor – hence its prevalence in our written regulations. On the other hand, our inability to address this ideal in a practical way is becoming a painful reminder of how stuck we are in our preference for those who are not really poor. Ironically, our close allegiance with the institutional Church(es) makes commitment to and solidarity with those who are really marginalised (e.g., women, outcasts, ethnic minorities) enormously difficult at times.

None the less, religious in the Christian tradition have been addressing this vow with a degree of openness and integrity which the vow for relatedness does not yet receive. They have moved away from the rather infantile practices of monitoring the use of every penny and dime, and are striving to live frugally, even within some of the most secure institutions that modern society has known. Either by choice or by fiscal obligation, many religious have parted with their large buildings and moved into smaller simpler residences located among the people. Many congregations have devised systems of budgeting and a financial structure in which every member is called to a participative adult form of accountability. Some congregations participate in ethical investment programmes and give serious attention to the justice implications of their financial investments. And, with the movement to smaller houses, many communities adopt a praxis and lifestyle which reflects the ecological challenge to 'live simply so that others can simply live'.

These developments are not so much about poverty as about responsible stewardship – hence the renaming of this vow recommended earlier. Poverty is an *evil* that should never be condoned nor exonerated. It erodes hope and meaning, and deprives millions all over our world from ever realising the fullness of their God-given potential. Material poverty underpins most other forms of deprivation that undermine the quality of personal and planetary life today. It is an intolerable sin in a world where there are more than adequate resources for all, if they were only distributed fairly and justly.

This is the global reality that engages the person vowed to stewardship: a painful awareness of the horrific injustices that create a world of 'haves' and 'have-nots', and then evokes a response that has three key dimensions to it:

a. Solidarity with the poor in the depth of their deprivation, injustice, pain, anger and frustration. Many religious in Latin and Central America attempt to make this quality of response with admirable courage and integrity.

b. Raising the consciousness of the poor on why they are poor and how they can begin to rectify it. Advocates of liberation theology, including substantial numbers of religious in Central and South America, strive to instigate this quality of witness, but encounter enormous opposition from political forces and from the Church, which tends to be aligned with the powerful, rather than with the weak. The struggle to respond authentically in terms of a process of consciousness-raising is expressed poignantly in the oft-quoted words of Helder Camara: 'If I give bread to the poor they call me a saint; if I ask why the poor have no bread they call me a communist'. As awareness-raisers especially in the pursuit of justice, Christian religious do not rate highly, but there has been marked increase in awareness and courageous praxis in the past few decades.

c. Confront and denounce prophetically the sinful systems that cause the poor to be poor in the first place. This is where religious are weakest. We do not have the socio-political skills nor the openness to political engagement, to make this happen. And the major blockage is the Christian Church itself, with its archaic dualism between the sacred and the secular (political), which discourages and prohibits religious from developing this immensely appropriate and urgent form of witness.

The liminal dimension of stewardship

Archetypally, the vow for stewardship is about a quality of engagement with the world and not a renunciation of it. It considers all creation, and all the goods of creation, to be God-given gifts, to be shared equally among all. The primary focus of the vow is the global interdependence whereby all the goods of creation are treated with the dignity and

115

respect deserving of any God-given gift. The vow for stewardship evokes a sense of *all* people being mutually responsible for how the gifts are used (e.g. are we humans automatically entitled to slaughter animals for our survival or to mine ruthlessly for mineral resources?). Not only are we accountable to God; we are also accountable to each other and to the planet we inhabit. The vow for stewardship cannot be lived authentically without strong recognition of its global, ecological and environmental dimensions.

All the vows have global ramifications, but, in a world facing imminent ecological catastrophe, none more directly than the vow for stewardship. The liminal call to stewardship involves pastoral outreach of a highly complex and urgent nature. We need to be deeply in tune with the pain of our world today, and become catalysts in raising people's consciousness regarding the route to perdition that our culture ruthlessly pursues. We need to become champions for justice in a world riddled with corruption and injustice.

In order to engage with the socio-political institutions and the multinational corporations which determine the unjust plight of billions (to the advantage of the few) we need to develop skills of political and social engagement unknown to previous generations and still anathema to the official Churches. In some cases the pacifist witness of a Mahatma Gandhi may be appropriate but in many others it is the courage, wisdom and endurance to engage with and reform the sinful political structures themselves.

To make all this possible we need to work initially at a shift in consciousness. All the religions still adhere heavily to a *personal* notion of sin, and we religious tend to adopt that same restrictive and misguided view. As liberation theologians have been stating for some 20 years now, *structural* and not *personal* sin is the major satanic force at work in our world today. It is the unjust and oppressive systems that exist all around us – even the Churches have their sinful structures – that drive many people to behave irresponsibly and immorally. This shift in awareness is itself a major undertaking. If religious did nothing else but take

116

that seriously, we would render our world a prophetic service of enormous import.

For the vowed person the call, therefore, to stewardship is one of critical and creative engagement with the use and abuse of the goods of creation, including Planet Earth itself. Our role is to model, on behalf of the people, those sustainable relationships that make justice and equality more attainable ideals. In a world where patriarchal interference has turned everything, including people, into objects to be conquered and controlled, our role is to reclaim the sacredness of all the goods of creation, which demands their use in a sharing, caring and interdependent mode. It is a daunting task, but one from which we must not shy away. Our own liminal integrity is at stake, but, more importantly, there is no meaningful future for humanity until our world adopts that radical sense of stewardship which the liminal people are called to activate and model on behalf of humanity.

The vow for partnership

Obedience features dominantly in all the major religions, and in most cases it is overtly hierarchical and patriarchal in its essence and structure. God is perceived to be the unconquered and unconquerable patriarch to whom we owe absolute and unquestioned obedience, before whom we present ourselves as totally subservient, passive and inferior. But between us and the supreme patriarch there exists a hierarchy wherein those at each level owe allegiance to those above them, culminating in a God-like figure at the top (pope, prime minister, president, major superior etc.), the prototype of which is a heroic male. Not infrequently, this supreme figurehead is perceived to be endowed with divine power (e.g., the king of old or the major superior in traditional religious orders); and in not a few cases the 'patriarch' attributed divine power to himself to validate or reinforce his wishes.

In this model, all power is invested in the person at the

top, whether it be God, the king, or the major superior of the religious order. Consequently, all those in subservient roles, no matter how holy, enlightened or gifted they may be, are divested – to one degree or another – of their God-given power. A genuine sharing of power is impossible in a patriarchal system, because patriarchy of its very nature breeds co-dependency, inequality and even the abuse of power. It is fundamentally a sinful system.

Patriarchy, in its present form as a dominant socio-political system, has been with us for at least 5,000 years. Its origins coincide with the upsurge of the Agricultural Revolution around 8,000 BCE, but it took some thousands of years to attain its current status. The rise of movements like Marxism and Socialism in the eighteenth century and the widespread adoption of democratic forms of government throughout the twentieth century, are just some of the cultural factors signalling the decline of patriarchy. But it was events like the student revolts of 1968, and other counter-cultural developments of the 1960s, that began to undermine patriarchy in a serious way. Today the feminist movement is emerging as the dominant alternative to this crumbling system which, confronted with its own demise, has become entrenched with a vengeance in religious and political circles alike.

The Christian Gospels display a strong anti-patriarchal bias, illustrated most graphically in the parable of the workers in the vineyard (Matt 20:1-16), where all are paid according to the norm of radical equality; or in the only scenario in the synoptic gospels in which Jesus allows himself to be called a king (Mk 11:1ff). He rides on a *donkey*, the ordinary people's beast of burden, and not on the royal kingly beast, the *horse*. Despite these unambiguous denunciations of patriarchy much of the New Testament has imbibed the dominant patriarchal value system. Moreover Christianity's early adoption of Greek culture, with its strongly dualistic perceptual and conceptual orientation, engraved the Christian religion with a patriarchal imprint that has prevailed to the present time.

The system of authority and obedience adopted by the vowed life emulates largely what was going on in the wider culture. Paradoxically the flight from the world nearly always leads to a more convoluted collusion with the world. Frequently in our Christian history, we religious become enmeshed in power games that diminish and camouflage our liminal marginality, subvert our prophetic contestation and alienate us from the very people to whom we are sent in mission. Our western marriage with the patriarchal socio-political system has led us into the exploitation and desecration of native cultures especially in Africa, and to collusions with western superpowers that made us perpetrators of heinous crimes against humanity. Today we find ourselves almost totally disempowered and unable to confront prophetically those sinful structures that reap such havoc in our world. We are unable to confront them, because we ourselves have been, and largely still are, enmeshed in those same structures.

In terms of the vowed life, what we traditionally called the vow of obedience has left us with a greater trail of disaster than either of the other vows. Generations have been indoctrinated with infantile submission; the desire to recreate a climate of accountability and co-responsibility is proving enormously difficult to initiate nor are our efforts helped in the Catholic tradition by the imposition of a canonical patriarchal superior in each community (household), who, in most male situations, has to be a clergyman.

The vow for partnership seeks to address the liminal challenge in the light of the new aspirations of our time. Our world is growing weary of patriarchy; it does not energise or animate us anymore. And at the socio-political level, it is clearly unable to address the urgent political, economic, ecological and social issues of our time. Only a fresh concerted effort, engaging people across all the traditional patriarchal dividing-lines of tribe, nation and religion, can address the critical questions confronting our world today. The rise of the United Nations in the late 1940s was a symbolic gesture in this direction, but, alas, it too has been jeopardised by the ruthless manipulation of the superpowers.

Liminal groups are called to name the new yearnings for more participative government and concerted leadership. They are also challenged to model, for the wider culture, processes of interaction that encourage and inculcate subsidiarity, co-reponsibility and mutual accountability. And from a Christian viewpoint, this means not just sharing power in new ways, but actually giving it away to empower and enable others to engage more fully in the divine-human task of co-creating our world anew.

Pastorally, Christian religious find themselves in a quandary. They are already deeply aware of these ideas, and strive to integrate them into their internal value systems. They also realise that the people among whom they live and minister also share these aspirations. But most religious in the Christian tradition still function within, or close to, the institutional Church which still heavily endorses the traditional patriarchal mode. How do we reconcile these divergent realities?

For a substantial number of religious, fired and enthused by a fresh sense of their liminal prophetic calling, there seems to be only one authentic response: leave the Church and adopt a non-canonical status. This has already begun to happen in the USA and in Latin America and is likely to become more extensive throughout the twenty-first century. There are also a substantial number of religious who in their hearts have outgrown the need for affiliation to the institutional Church (as is the case for millions of contemporary Christians), although they have not formally left. These realities prove painful and burdensome for some; others use their creativity and imagination to find ways to circumvent this dilemma.

For many religious the most immediate challenge is the task of addressing the unjust and oppressive patriarchy of the Church itself and subsequently diverting attention to the justice agenda of the wider world. This may not be an appropriate nor responsible liminal option. The religious

RESUME OF THE PASTORAL FRAME

COMMUNITY LIFE

Facilitating a process of interaction at the interpersonal and collective levels, for the purposes of exploring and mediating the social, spiritual and ritual dimensions of the human need for meaning and wholeness.

THE VOW FOR RELATEDNESS

Engaging afresh with the central questions and issues of our time in the human desire to relate more intimately and authentically, especially in the psychosexual realm.

THE VOW FOR STEWARDSHIP

Challenging the attitudes, values and structures whereby the goods of creation are selfishly horded, thus inflicting poverty and exploitation upon millions all over the earth. Justice for, and solidarity with, the poor are inherent to this task.

THE VOW FOR PARTNERSHIP

Naming critical issues of our time around power and powerlessness; undermining the dominance of patriarchy and its oppressive impact on people and on the environment; invoking new ways of sharing both power and powerlessness.

life calling is to and for the world, and not just for the sake of the Church. Entrenched institutions are often so resistant to change that they are better left to decline and become extinct. Meanwhile, the call of our time may be to shift one's energy and attention to the world, where God's creative Spirit breathes openly and freely, inviting us to the transformative task of renewing all things in Christ. This, I suggest is where the vow for partnership takes on the greatest significance for our time; this is where the prophetic liminal people need to relocate their presence and unique giftedness.

The locus for pastoral witness

Our consideration of the three vows raises the urgent question of where we religious should locate ourselves and our resources, if we are to engage meaningfully and creatively with the world of our time. Throughout the post-Tridentine era we have been co-opted into the institutional Church. Today we find ourselves largely within the Church and increasingly bewildered by the stifling feeling of that ambience. Deep in our hearts we know we are meant to be about something more than just the concerns of the Church. We are part of a larger reality, of a more global vocation. This is our liminal conscience, prodding us on to fresh pastures. Where do we turn for wisdom and guidance?

Throughout the post-Tridentine era we turned to bishops and priests, often in a diocesan context. After about 1960 we tended to look to the Sacred Congregation for religious (SCRSI) in Rome. In both cases we were falling into the trap of co-dependent children seeking the guidance and approbation of dysfunctional parents, both groups being locked into a dysfunctional (sinful) system. The only way to break that vicious cycle is for somebody to step out of it; and that tends to be the privileged challenge of youth, unless of course they are so de-skilled and disempowered that fear will inhibit them, too, from taking the risk.

This is only one of many risks that accompany the reframing of religious life for the future. Indeed, risk-taking itself is one of the most frequently occurring pastoral issues we encounter today. If we are to be truly liminal in our mission to and for people we too must take the risks without which we lack true meaning and integrity. In moving out of the institutional Church we are not abandoning the people; quite the opposite – we are seeking to pitch our tent where the people are and where they engage daily with the human-divine struggle to grow and to be wise, to learn and to love.

And this, too, is where our accountability belongs: *with the people*. It is the people who bring us into being not the Church, nor the Sacred Congregation for religious. It is to God and to the people that we render an account of our stewardship. Whether consciously or unconsciously, it is the people who will judge us in the end: and, depending on the verdict, our future destiny is renewed or declared redundant. Our destiny is in the hands of that divine-human co-creativity which brings us into being, sets us forth in mission and revitalises our potential for the ever-fresh challenges of our planet and our world. We survive for as long as we serve a purpose greater than ourselves, and that very destiny is not about survival, but about the call to mission which espouses something akin to the fullness of life which all Christians (indeed all humans) are invited to embrace.

CHAPTER SEVEN

Reframing for the twenty-first century: Towards a new paradigm

The future is always more original than our thinking of it. A blueprint for the future is not the same as a vision of it... Only a new meaning can reconstitute Religious Life.

Mary Jo Leddy

The dawn of a new millennium brings the predictable mixture of hope and trepidation. We anticipate that the waves of change will continue to sweep across our world, gaining greater momentum and rapidity. At times this feels immensely exciting and energising, but frequently we feel we are being swept along by forces which could so easily overwhelm us.

We have reduced the threat of nuclear annihilation; we have raised standards of health-care, education and literacy; we have forged communication networks that now include the remotest corners of the globe, and since 1950 we have established democratic political processes in every one of the great continents.

And yet the rich continue to exploit the poor with greater viciousness and sophistication. We still stockpile armaments that could destroy Planet Earth not once but one hundred times over, costing an annual budget that could feed the entire human population for an estimated ten years. The pollution and environmental destruction continues unabated and, perhaps most frightening of all, western governments become increasingly inept and unable to comprehend or address the major socio-political issues of our time.

These are the *signs of the times* that engage our attention as we stand on the threshold of a new millennium. What

124

have we Religious to say to this world? How do we dialogue with it, understand it and respond from within our liminal prophetic context? Can we even begin to comprehend that the *world* is the arena, and *the only authentic one* in which our prophetic agenda is activated? Can we internalise our call to mission, not just for the sake of the Church, but for the world of our time, perched between the peril and promise of new possibilities?

Striving to connect

None of us can predict what the new millennium will evoke for humanity and for Planet Earth. One thing is certain, however: *horizons will continue to expand.* Evolution moves predominantly in one direction: forward (despite the many temporary setbacks of the evolutionary story). And with the forward movement there is growth in creativity and complexity. The nature of understanding itself will continue to shift from the focus on breaking everything down into tiny units (the deductive approach of classical mechanistic science) to that of relating with the *total* context of reality, in which each part is perceived within the greater whole to which it belongs – the wholistic approach, the significance of which I explore at length in O'Murchu (1996).

The transition from the mechanistic to the holistic highlights among other things the demise of patriarchy, the masculine-based value system that has dominated our world for the past 10,000 years now clinging on to the last vestiges of life with inflexible rigidity and ferocious denial. It is at the political and religious levels more than any others, that the patriarchal will to power still prevails. As these systems continue to crumble – as they inevitably will – forces of anarchy and chaos will be unleashed. In that painful and destructive Calvary-moment we will encounter once more the greatest paradox of all: only in death can new life unfold.

Where will we Religious be at that precarious and prophetic moment? On the hill of Calvary, alongside those bewildered, confused women who stood there until the bitter end (cf. Lk 23:55) or alongside the apostles, who fled in fear because their patriarchal world was being shattered to pieces? And when it comes to Easter morning – as all four Gospels illustrate graphically – it was those same women who were there to encounter the resurrected one; and despite their fear and pain (to which all the Gospels allude) they were able to make the connection of meaning. Had the women not been able to make that connection one wonders if the apostles would ever have grasped the real meaning of resurrection.

Reframing religious life for the twenty-first century poses a double challenge: humanitarian and planetary. Effectively these are two sides of the one coin. Can we connect deeply with the unfolding human story of our time, with its deep incarnational yearnings, at this hour of transition? In the patriarchal culture humans were perceived to be *masters* of creation (cf. Gen 1:28), but we do not find that type of language (or consciousness) anywhere in the New Testament; Christians are called to be *stewards* of all that is entrusted to their care. In the post-patriarchal world we are invited to shed our manipulative anthropocentrism; to assume our unique but *participatory* role among all the other life-forms that comprise the grand landscape of creation. We humans – women and men alike – need to let go of the masculine will to power, domination and control; instead we are invited to assume and internalise a sense of being co-creators with our creative God in an essentially creative universe. We need to learn to flow with the experience of life, not to direct, dominate, or control it.

In that capacity we are called to be *midwives* (see Conlon 1990) to the unfolding creative process, and we need visionaries (not experts) to model that role for us. This is where liminal people really come into their own. This is where the alternative prophetic imagination flowers and flourishes. Can we religious of the twenty-first century rise to this challenge and become the catalysts for re-inventing the incarnational challenge of becoming new people, to assume a new role in our post-patriarchal age?

Our planetary vocation

Secondly, our new sense of vocation includes among other things, a capacity to relate to Planet Earth (and to all other life-forms) in a subject-to-subject relationship and not in a subject-object liaison as we currently do. This is the new planetary agenda; new for our time, but not new in terms of the evolutionary story itself. We need to reclaim the ancient wisdom which perceived Planet Earth as a living organism, a mother that nurtures and nourishes all her creatures with fierce love and protectiveness, a creature of indomitable endurance who can – in the long term – overcome the destructive impact of those who inappropriately interfere, and whom one day she may choose to replace with a more benevolent species.

Already in contemporary spirituality, ecological concerns loom large. It is not just a matter of including environmental considerations among a host of other demands. It is a great deal more than that. The eco-spiritual undercurrent is drawing us towards a paradigm shift of enormous cultural and spiritual import. It is challenging us to envisage the planet as the primary life-force within which each of us is a constituent part. We belong to a reality greater than ourselves not merely to a God beyond the world, but more immediately to a co-creative God whose body is that of the universe itself (cf. McFague 1993). This is incarnation in its fuller meaning: God becomes human, not in outer space or in some heavenly realm, but right in the heart of creation itself. Immanuel is the God with us; when will we choose to reciprocate in a truly incarnational way?

Acquaintance, therefore, with planetary and ecological issues is not just a fad for our time that religious could beneficially appropriate. No, these issues are central to the

127

very meaning of our lives as religious. We are invited to be the cultural catalysts for these new global and spiritual engagements. We must outgrow our dualistic thought-forms, our alienation from the world, our often sectarian allegiance to one or other religious system. We are moving within a world of rapidly expanding horizons. This is fertile territory for liminal and prophetic witness; if we Religious abdicate that responsibility, others will be missioned to take our place!

In 1978 the Catholic Church issued the document *Mutuae Relationes* with a view to improving relations between religious and bishops. At an international conference on religious life in Rome (November 1993), many participants asked for a fresh rendition of that document. This is a good example of patching up an old wineskin when in fact it is a totally new one that is needed. The key issue is no longer about improved relationships with Churches or formal religions but about right relationships with a rapidly evolving world. Liminal movements that seek their identity within formal institutions quickly lose their capacity to be liminal and their duty to be prophetic. Their true place is the open arena of God's universe – at the heart of the world where the New Reign of God continues to unfold. When the liminars choose to centre themselves in the world they will not have abandoned the Church; hopefully they will have reclaimed their duty to be the dangerous memory that shocks the Church (cf. Metz 1978) into realising that she too is meant to be at the heart of the world, as the living community that heralds and celebrates God's New Reign of justice, love, peace and liberation.

Prospects of refounding

So what kind of future are we Religious likely to reweave as we embrace the new world of the twenty-first century? In the Christian story we are at a painful place on the downward slant of the cyclic historical model. The missionary cycle commenced around 1800 CE and peaked around 1960, when there were some 1.4 million religious in the Christian Churches; their number has dwindled to now a little less than 900,000. Influentially, pastorally and culturally, we are also forced to assume a significantly diminished role. Many orders and congregations today exhibit the precarious characteristics of what Meyer and Zucker (1989) call *permanently failing institutions*. As the missionary cycle completes its course in the latter half of the twenty-first century, we can expect many currently extant groups to become extinct. In due course, as we move into the twenty-second century, we can expect a new cycle to unfold, and with it another golden era for the monastic and religious life.

The realisation that we live in one of those times, demoralised by our diminishing impact and yearning for fresh life and vitality, has led one writer to explore the notion of *refounding* the vowed life (Arbuckle 1986; 1988; 1993). Arbuckle delineates five main stages in the refounding process:

a. Members of an order or congregation are experiencing the confusion and malaise of chaos; i.e., risking to enter into the death experience.

b. The group (or at least an unspecified proportion) acknowledges that new life will not emanate from the old model, but from within a totally new paradigm. In Arbuckle's own words: 'The new is elsewhere'.

c. Acknowledging their own powerlessness to do anything about the chaos, religious (and especially their leaders) strive to be as open as possible to the new call from God in the context of urgent contemporary needs.

d. Leaders release 'prophetic' members (highly creative and visionary) to pursue the new possibilities.

e. Some will be motivated enough to follow the new

vision, and those that cannot will die with the old reality. In time, the new vision becomes the refounded order or congregation, which effectively means it is founded again at a new starting point.

Initially, the notion of refounding inspired great enthusiasm, and workshops on the subject attracted large numbers all over the Christian world. It sounded like an idea that was right for its time, a lifeline that many wanted to grasp. In a short time the idea lost its impetus, along with much of its initial energy and widespread appeal. Some reasons are clear, others less so:

1. The initial vision was hyped up with euphoria and false expectation. Some thought the refounding process could commence almost immediately, and produce fresh life and possibilities in a short number of years.
2. Although Arbuckle contextualized the refounding process within the breakdown of an old system (the chaos), somehow or other people did not grasp that crucial paschal dimension. Traditional groups hoped that new life could be activated, while still resourcing their former commitments. People were hoping for a resurrection without having to undergo a Calvary.
3. Although many warmed to the notion of the new being elsewhere, few seemed to grasp the transitional struggle of having to leave the 'old' behind in order to move towards the new unencumbered by archaic baggage.
4. Although Arbuckle can evoke many historical precedents for his proposition of key refounding *individuals* he underplays the critical role that discerning *community* plays in that process.
5. The theory of refounding often lacked appropriate historical contextualisation. The fact that religious life generally is on a downward cyclic slope leads to an overwhelming conviction that refounding in any serious sense is unlikely for at least another 70 years.
6. An unquestioned assumption seemed to prevail that

we religious would refound ourselves. At every stage in the history of religious life, founding and refounding have been the fruit of divine, and not human initiative. Admittedly, it always takes place through people – not necessarily those ready and waiting – but often those, like the Old Testament prophets, unprepared and unwilling, but none the less open to be surprised by our co-creative God.

Refounding is a notion for the twenty-first century, which by accident or design has fallen into the twentieth century. And therein lies a grace that we need to embrace with openness and faith. What the notion – and its enormous challenge – poses for us is a stark reminder of how stuck many of us are in the old paradigm, and how difficult it is, and will be, for us to move our tents. If there is not among us a radical openness to *experimentation*, how can we ever hope to be refounded, if that is God's will for us? And although refounding is a divine prerogative, I believe that Arbuckle is correct in suggesting that it will happen primarily for those who can befriend the chaos and confusion of our time and be converted to respond in totally new ways to the needs of our unfolding world. The concept of refounding may seem to be premature, but its underlying message must not go unheeded.

While many religious have explored the dynamics of the refounding process, relatively few seem to have converted to its underlying spirituality, which is what validates and authenticates its theory. The notion is firmly rooted in the paschal experience of death and resurrection. There can be no new life without a dying, a letting go of all that we have loved and cherished. And there is no meaningful rationale – human or divine – to explain the chaos and confusion of Calvary. Why Jesus had to die such an ignominious, barbaric death as a prerequisite for resurrection remains an eternal paradox which Jesus himself did not even attempt to explain. Nor can we rationally comprehend the discontinuity between Calvary and resurrection succinctly captured in the jolting statement of the messengers

131

at the tomb: 'Why seek the living among the dead?' (Lk 24:5). It was a logical thing to do but we are dealing with something here that is much larger than logic. Yes, resurrection-possibility is *elsewhere* in Galilee (cf. Matt 28:7) where Jesus initially proclaimed the New Reign of God.

We religious stand on the threshold of a confusing and exciting world. This may not be a time for refounding. Our challenge is to befriend the dark and the dying, the pregnancy pains and the various struggles to bring life to birth. This is an hour for contemplative waiting of a type succinctly versed in the *Four Quartets* of T.S. Eliot:

> I said to my soul be still and wait without hope
> For hope would be hope for the wrong thing;
> Wait without love
> For love would be love for the wrong thing.
> There is yet faith.
> But the faith and the love and hope are all in the
>   waiting.
> Wait without thought for you are not ready
>   for thought.
> So the darkness shall be the light
> And the stillness the dancing!

No greater grace do we need at this time than the ability to be still... and wait! – a recurring theme in Fiand (1996). Hopefully, the reflections of this book, if we allow them to stretch our imaginations and pierce open our hearts anew, will predispose us afresh to the still voice within. From within that creative solitude we will hear the cries of a new millennium, and from within our evolving universe renewed echoes of the divine-human invitation: Come follow me!

CHAPTER EIGHT:

What about the ecclesiastical frame?

It is our turn now – if religious life is really the pro-
phetic dimension of the Church – to be willing to be
strangers in our own land, to be willing to stay where
we do not fit, to be committed to say what is not wel-
come to be heard...

Joan D. Chittister.

In the Christian Church the relationship of religious life to
the official Church has rarely been one of mutual benefit.
The Church has claimed the right to examine, approve,
monitor and control its various charismatic elements, including the vowed life, while religious orders and congregations, even when firmly rooted in the ecclesiastical
tradition, have sought a measure of autonomy and self-
governance. Since the Council of Trent in the sixteenth
century, Religious have been so absorbed into mainstream
Catholicism that for many the vowed life is inconceivable
outside of an ecclesial or ecclesiastical context.[12]

Post-Tridentine Developments

This absorption of the post-Tridentine era requires a thorough critique far beyond my competence or in the space
allowed in this book. The informed reader will realise that
the Council of Trent was Catholicism's comprehensive
defence against the onslaught of the Protestant Reforma-
tion. The sanctity, sacramentality and power of the Church
were vehemently reasserted, and to ensure the rigorous
implementation of this new vision the *male, white, celibate*
cleric began to assume a leading ideological role, one that
has dominated Catholicism ever since.

By vesting it's power and vision in the male, white, celibate cleric, Trent undermined rather than enhanced the true meaning of Christian priesthood (as a ministry of *service*). More significantly, for the present work, it exalted the "ideal cleric" to be the model for all Christians, religious included. Religious – women in particular – were required to be totally subservient to the value-system and dictates of the clericalised Church. And as the guidelines of Trent assumed canonical status, clerics (especially Bishops) were permitted, indeed obliged, to interfere in even the minutest details on how the vowed life should be structured and lived out. The liminal prophetic movement was essentially reduced to another *structure* of the institutional Church.

In the eyes of the people, religious were perceived to belong to the "sacred" dimension of ecclesiastical life. The special call to holiness was deemed to be superior to that of the people of God; consequently, the call to liminality was misconstrued and, in time, largely eroded. Religious within the Church were considered to be in full harmony with the value-system of clericalism, to such an extent that Sisters were obliged to don a predominately black and white clericalised dress, while Brothers, who dressed almost identically to priests, were often perceived and treated as unsuitable for, or incapable of, being ordained to the priesthood.

The deviations perpetuated by this misguided system, while facilitating some admirable holiness and unstinting apostolic service, has, nonetheless, had devastating effects on thousands of women and men, and has proved enormously destructive to the deeper meaning of the monastic and religious life.

For contemporary religious, the ecclesiastical frame of reference continues to be of central importance and therein lies one of the great dilemmas facing the vowed life today. In fact we have been conformed and domesticated to a degree that has all but usurped our potential for liminal witness and for prophetic contestation. Even when these elements are recognised and attempts are made to (re)activate them the focus remains – largely or exclusively – on the Church. The notion that religious life can have meaning and significance apart from the official Church is virtually inconceivable for most religious (a line adopted by Billy 1993).

This strong Church-centredness may be considered a weakness rather than a strength. It usually betrays a poorly informed understanding of religious life – culturally, historically and theologically defective. Often the wider cultural context explored in this book is absent; many religious are not even aware of it. Even the richly complex historical unfolding within the Christian version is scarcely appreciated, while theologically the focus on *Church*, rather than on the *New Reign of God*, condemns religious to a stultifying and debilitating sense of mission and identity.

Pastorally, the close liaison with the official Church often alienates us from those very people whom we feel the call to accompany in a special way. I refer to the millions of marginalised women and men for whom the Church no longer offers either meaning or hope; or the millions who feel they have outgrown the need for formal religion but still search for spiritual meaning. In many cases we encounter these people and engage more dynamically with them outside, rather than within, an ecclesiastical context.

Beyond the Ecclesiastical Referent

The option not to include a chapter on the ecclesiastical frame of reference is intended in no way to bypass or underestimate the close link that most religious have had, and wish to retain, with the official Church. But at this moment of profound transition in religious life we need to reconnect with the deeper layers that impinge upon the meaning and purpose of our existence. We need to reconnect with deep roots, with those well-springs where the waters (of tradition) are purest.

The late B.C. Butler, auxiliary Bishop of London, on returning from the Second Vatican Council, wrote the following words:

> But few of us seemed to have very clear or distinct ideas about the theology of religious life; or if we did they proved singularly out of harmony with the general theological renewal that was taking shape within the Council itself. In default of a good and dynamic theology our temptation seemed to be to take refuge behind the bastions of Canon Law.

In a sense, this is the heart of our dilemma: the real essence of religious life has been whittled away amid a plethora of canonical impositions. The archetypal value-radiation which, I suggest, is our primary theological and pastoral raison d'être has been reduced to a legalistic structure incapable of sustaining or energising us for the real work that we are meant to be about at the heart of creation. Our ecclesiastical ambience, despite all the rhetoric of "cherishing" and "supporting" our vocation, in reality continues to undermine what is *unique* about that vocation. Our special place within the Church, the close *communion* advocated by the 1994 Synod on Religious Life (see *Vita Consecrata* 1996, pp. 42-57) impoverishes rather than enriches the meaning and purpose of our existence. Precisely because religious life now finds itself in crisis, it can no longer take comfort in, nor guidance from, answers that distract from our essential reality as a cultural, liminal movement. This time of transition is for us, as for millions in today's world, a dislocating time in which standard values (laws) and approaches simply do not work. Many panic and opt out, but for those who choose to remain we know we must search more deeply for a faith to sustain us. It is precisely out of this option – to reconnect with the deeper story – we are once more discovering the core meaning of the monastic and religious life. And for many the unexpected paradox of that discovery is the fresh call to reclaim the *world* and not the *Church* as the primary context of our life and witness.

Reclaiming our mission at the heart of the world does not in itself mean denial or rejection of our alliance with the Church. What it does necessitate is a very different way of being Church, a development that has as much to contribute to the life of the Church as it has to religious life itself. The experience of Church that can accommodate and respect our liminal, prophetic uniqueness is that of the believing community which seeks to integrate and celebrate the diversity of gifts (charisms) bestowed upon our world for the sake of God's New Reign at the heart of creation.

A Church that seeks to be servant and herald of the New Reign of God remains open and porous to human and planetary yearnings; it seeks to engage with people in their struggles to relate to life with greater love, justice, peace and liberation. And it is not particularly concerned with its own survival, because it believes that it is God's New Reign and not the Church itself, that eventually endures.

All over the Christian world today, religious women and men struggle with their allegiance to the Church. Intuitively, many feel that they have outgrown the need for that institution which distorts their vision (as in the hassle about the approval of constitutions), fails to comprehend their dreams, jeopardises their creativity and stymies their desire to journey more closely with the pilgrim people. For increasing numbers, the call to engage prophetically with the world outweighs the legalism and protectionism of a Church often perceived to be out of touch with the real world of our time. For religious, there often ensues the painful choice between going where life is, or remaining stuck in decadence and irrelevancy.

Reclaiming our sacred story

While dialogue with the Church needs to continue, there is an urgently felt need for religious themselves to reclaim their own story, and take on those daring and controversial initiatives that will reground a more authentic vision for the sake of the *world*. Inevitably this will lead to a degree of diversity and pluriformity which contemporary Church leadership is highly unlikely to consider, never mind accept.

For many religious today dialogue with the official church is so difficult to attain that negotiation seems totally unrealisable. Rather than waste precious time, energy and resourcefulness with what is often perceived to be an alien and alienating institution, increasingly religious find themselves drawn to the urgent and overwhelming call to mission at the heart of the world; faced with that call it would be sinful not to respond, irrespective of whether the Church approves or not.

Contemporary religious are also beginning to explore and articulate a fresh sense of Christian commitment, one that often baffles people involved in formation and leadership, and indeed substantial numbers, too, among the rank and file of our orders and congregations. The old dualistic distinction of being either *in* the Church or *outside* it no longer resonates with pastoral experience. I may choose to opt out of official commitment in terms of ecclesiastical structure (e.g., parish), or even desist from sacramental practice, but every time I engage with people in their struggle to create a world characterised by love, justice, peace and liberation I am engaging in the work of God's New Reign on earth. When that struggle leads towards the desire for, and exploration of, meaningful community (even on a purely "secular" level like creating a workers' co-operative) then I am encountering the God who is present where two or three are gathered in his/her name. These engagements, I suggest, are biblically and genuinely *ecclesial*, without necessarily being *ecclesiastical*. I am *being Church* with and for people, irrespective of my commitment to *the* Church.

There may be, therefore, something deeply prophetic in the desire among increasing numbers of religious to adopt a *non-canonical* status. In many cases it is neither a com-

fortable nor irresponsible cop-out, but a positive and courageous option to safeguard and foster what is truly unique
about the vowed life, namely its unflinching allegiance to
the work of God at the heart of the world, especially on the
side of those alienated and excluded by formal institutions
including the Church itself. The liminal prophetic option is
becoming quite volatile once more, and offers the brightest
and strongest hope for the future of religious life.

Opting out or moving beyond ?

The reframing of religious life suggested in this book does
not require the Church as overall guardian, nor even as an
essential ingredient. The vowed life makes complete sense
in itself, apart entirely from that ecclesiastical context in
which millions assume it must be grounded. Religious life
predates the Christian Church and all the formal religions
known to us today by thousands of years; religious life
values belong to an even more ancient pre-religious tradition. These are our deep roots; this is our ancient story, ever
old and ever new; this is our sacred tradition, of which no
movement or organisation should deprive us. Nor should
we permit such watering down and domestication to take
place; our service to the world will be the poorer if we do.

The domestication of the vowed life by official churches
and formal religions is a major obstacle to the refounding
of religious life as a liminal, prophetic movement of and
for the people, at the heart of the world. The landscape of
our mission is more extensive and enduring than any religion or church ever has been, or hopes to be. Ours is a
different agenda, not a superior one, but complementary.
We are about archetypal (universally shared) values, mediated through liminal structures and through prophetic contestation.[13] What we are about is not alien to the deeper
vision of the churches or the religions.

The fundamental values which the churches and the
religions seek to activate and mediate are precisely those

139

entrusted to liminal and prophetic movements, and the latter take on an enormously difficult role (which they must not shy away from) when the formal religious institutions exalt their own status to the cost of the deeper values – which is very much the religious crisis confronting our world today.

In suggesting, therefore, that Christian religious life reclaims its legitimate liminal space *beyond* (rather than *outside*) institutionalised Christianity, I am not suggesting that it also shuns the biblical vision of that faith. As explored in chapter four, there is a Christian theology within which the vowed life, in its liminal and prophetic mission, makes a great deal of sense. That theological focus is not about *Church*, however, but about the *New Reign of God (Kingdom)*. In this new theological context, religious are invited to reclaim the world as the landscape for mission and witness. Herein their accountability is not to the Church but to the entire people of God, wherever right relationships of love, justice, peace and liberation are being worked out.

At the present time, it is inconceivable that these reflections will even be heard in formal ecclesiastical circles. In so far as they are the yearnings arising from the hearts of religious women and men around the world, they need to be articulated, spoken aloud and named. They contain fundamental truths that cannot be erased from the collective psyche; they touch the very heart of our vocation and existence, and, consequently, they will continue to demand attention and recognition in all future discernments about the meaning and purpose of the vowed life.

In this age of transition, more than at any other time, we need to be rooted in that ancient wisdom, which survives crises and begets fresh possibilities to reincarnate the ever-old in a world that is ever new. The more rooted we are in our past, the greater our chances of being born anew.

CHAPTER NINE:

Spirituality for a time of reframing

The human heart can go the lengths of God.
Dark and cold we may be, but this
Is no winter now. The frozen misery
Of centuries breaks, cracks, begins to move.
The thunder is the thunder of the floes,
The thaw, the flood, the upstart Spring.
Thank God, our time is now, when wrong
Comes up to face us everywhere,
Never to leave us till we take
The longest stride of soul people ever took.
Affairs are now soul-size;
The enterprise is exploration into God.
Where are you making for? It takes
So many thousand years to wake,
But will you wake, for pity's sake?

Christopher Fry

'Affairs are now soul-size...' And so is *spirituality*! For long assumed to be a by-product of formal religion, with a specific concern for the individual's relationship with God, spirituality now finds itself lured into a multi-disciplinary dialogue around the perennial global questions of our time. What was one time considered to be the reserve of the monastery (and the enclosed convent) has largely broken through those dualisms that separate the sacred from the secular, and is now emerging as the *bridge-builder* across the several divides that have alienated people from one another and from God.

Of all the reframings suggested in this book, the reframing of spirituality presents the most original and provocative challenge for our time. The spiritual landscape now expands across all the religions inviting humans to a new sense of convergence around the critical questions facing humanity today. This is not the naive syncretism that preoccupies some multi-faith theologians, nor is it in any way a reductionistic relativism that betrays the uniqueness of Jesus for Christian believers (questions explored at length in Knitter 1995). What we experience today is a major paradigm shift, inviting us to shed the accretions of the past few thousand years (many of which are religious in nature) and reclaim a more primordial and globally-centred vision which considers all humans (and creation itself) to be fundamentally spiritual in nature (For further elucidation, see O'Murchu 1997).

Many women and men in vowed commitment are aware of this new development; and they struggle to integrate it into their lives and ministries. Frequently, it is a difficult undertaking, burdened as we are with a great deal of spiritual baggage from the past which religious are expected to uphold and foster. Religious closely associated with formal Church or religion often feel torn between this traditional allegiance and the immediacy of the growing reality in people's lives asking different questions around spiritual meaning – requiring very different answers from those of bygone days.

The new spiritual ferment, while exciting and potentially full of promise, is often experienced as a perilous journey, open to many tensions and misunderstandings. A great deal of trust, dialogue and informed awareness is required if we, religious, are to engage meaningfully with this moment of hope and promise.

Spirituality and our theological synthesis

The reframing explored in this book provides a new synthesis for a revitalised theology of Religious Life. The synthesis itself is incomplete without that quality of spiritual connectedness that enables us to understand and appropriate how the various elements act as a creative whole, and how they can best be integrated into our lives and ministries. A renewal of our spiritual vision is at the heart of a revitalised theology of the vowed life.

The diagram on p. 144 highlights the key constituents of this emerging theology and the unfolding pattern in which these elements interact in the lived experience of religious themselves. There are four central concepts: *Mission* (the 'why'); *Liminality* (the 'where'); *Archetypal Values* (the 'what') and *Prophetic Witness* (the 'how'). The spiritual challenge for religious themselves, and their authentic response to the great spiritual questions of our age, cannot be fully realised without incorporating – in theory and in practice – all the elements of this synthesis.

1. *Mission.* This is our starting point, the foundational inspiration for any authentic vocation, Christian or otherwise. Mission refers to that outward orientation, towards people and our world as bearers and catalysts of Good News. For Christians, the spring-board and primary inspiration for this undertaking is the New Reign of God (the Kingdom) which we explored in Chapter Four. Spurred on by this vision, we are *sent* into the world. We don't choose to go, simply or solely on our own initiative.

The call of the Kingdom requires an availability for service, for risk, for engagement, an option to befriend all who are condemned to being 'non-persons', deprived of the inclusive and empowering love of God. The ultimate rationale for this task is beyond the immediate grasp of the human mind. In rational terms we can never fully explain this attraction; if we did so, we would have explained it away and thus stripped our vocation of it's innate spiritual meaning.

For Christians, the sending out is consciously linked to the life and ministry of Jesus. What Christians perceive as being unique to their faith tradition is, in fact, shared by millions the world over in the universal yearning (often subconscious rather than conscious) to live according to the gospel values of justice, love, peace and liberation.

While mission strongly denotes a sense of being sent out, it should not be identified solely with *ministry*. The quality of life-style that nourishes people for ministry, and becomes the focus for discernment on apostolic needs, options and approaches, is of equal importance, because without it, ministry can all too easily becomes a form of activism motivated primarily by achievement or job-satisfaction, rather than by the call to be transformative agents of God's New Reign in the world.

THE PATTERN FOR POSSIBILITIES

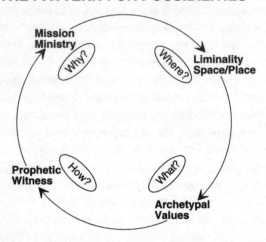

2. *Liminality*. This refers to the 'space' in which God invites us to activate the counter-cultural dimension of our mission. In itself, this is not an anti-world stance, characterised by separation and marginality, an understanding that prevailed in centuries past. As explained in Chapter Three, ours is a form of marginalisation on behalf of the world and its peoples. bell hooks (1991, p.153), reflecting on her role as a black feminist theologian, expresses succinctly and creatively what the liminal call is about:

I make a definite distinction between that marginality which is opposed by oppressive structures and that marginality one chooses as a site of resistance – as a location of radical openness and possibility. This site of resistance is continually formed in that segregated culture of opposition that is our critical response to domination. We are transformed individually and collectively as we make radical creative space which affirms and sustains our subjectivity, which gives us a new location from which to articulate our sense of the world. The choice for the margin is for the purpose of transforming the centre.

The location for liminal witness may in itself have consequences for geographical location (place). Witnessing to gospel values of justice and simplicity of lifestyle is incongruent with opulence and the appropriation of the standards and norms of the rich and powerful. Equally and increasingly precarious is our close identification with mainstream church and formal religion. When religious are perceived to be in close partnership with clergy or with religious devotees, this correspondingly inhibits the capacity for liminal witness among the millions who have no affiliation to church or religion. Our liminal vocation is an invitation to be present to *all* God's people and not just to those committed to church or religion.

How we, religious, reclaim our liminal space, and how we incarnate it in the context of the contemporary world, confronts us with the greatest single challenge as we move into the new millennium. The quality and quantity of former spiritualities are unlikely to reassure us for that undertaking. A more creative and comprehensive approach is urgently needed.

3. *Archetypal Values*. Contrary to an earlier understanding of religious life, the liminal witness is not for the sanctification or perfection of the liminal people themselves, but for the articulation and negotiation of those foundational values to which all humans aspire. *Value-radiation*, on behalf of all God's people, is the raison d'être of the vowed life. *Values* and not *laws* provide the infrastructure for our life and witness.

145

The priority of *law* over *value* has contributed in no small way to the current crisis in spirituality. Over recent years, spirituality evolved (or perhaps devolved) amid a plethora of obligations and prohibitions. In time, moralism, legalism and ritualism usurped the creative engagement with spiritual energy and creativity. Consequently, many people became confused and disheartened in the desperate attempt to measure up to the religious 'rights and wrongs', often abandoning their innate spiritual resourcefulness to cope and engage more creatively with life.

Culturally, too, we have evolved a world view, fragmented and torn between the dualism of the sacred and the secular. Creation itself, our primary and primordial source of divine revelation, has itself been de-sacralized and devalued. The value of patriarchal domination, with its ruthless philosophy of 'divide and conquer' has infiltrated every sphere of life, the religions included. Reclaiming or sacred and long-lost *relational* and *egalitarian* values will be a momentous task – which at this precarious stage of human evolution may even require the extinction of Homo Sapiens itself (more on this controversial topic in O'Murchu 1997, 141-156).

4. *Prophetic Witness*. Finally, we reconnect with the material of Chapter Two, highlighting that special quality of witness required by the liminal people to incarnate and negotiate our foundational values. The nature of this witness is summarily stated by Joan Chittister (1995, p.144):

> The religious voice must be a voice that brings to the public debate the best in tradition, the finest in theological analysis, the keenest in social perception and the most challenging of gospel values.

The prophetic call is not merely a *denunciation* of those values that alienate humans and creation from the call of the Gospel and that undermine our innate capacity for value-appropriation. More importantly, it *enunciates* the alternative values that need to be awakened, the alternative structures that need to be developed, and the alternative imagination that needs to be evoked if we are to engage courageously and creatively with God's New Reign in the world of our time.

The Power to Connect

The diagram on page 144 illustrates the interactive elements that brings religious life alive in the richness and complexity of its unfolding story. It also suggests that religious life is open to several historical expressions, as the new circumstances of time and culture require. Indeed, the durability of any one model largely depends on its adaptability, flexibility, creativity and spiritual versatility.

The versatility I refer to is the power to connect, which I wish to suggest is the core element of any viable spirituality, and the dimension that we are striving to reclaim afresh in the spiritual upsurge of our time. The feminist theologian, Charlene Spretnak describes spirituality as '...the aspect of human existence that explores the subtle forces of energy in and around us and reveals to us profound interconnectedness' (quoted in Raphael 1996, p. 226).

This power is not unique to human beings, but in fact underpins creation at large throughout the length, breadth and depth of its evolutionary story. The capacity to relate, to behave in an interdependent and interconnected way is the oldest and most enduring of all spiritual values. We encounter it in the behaviour of the sub-atomic world, in the tripartite structure that dominates terrestrial life (cf. Greenstein 1988) and even in the foundational imprint of the curvature of space-time itself. (cf. Swimme & Berry 1992).

For those who have developed a more contemplative mode of perception and apprehension, this interconnectedness is far more apparent in the various life-forms that populate our earth, than in the adversarial, competitive and destructive behaviour that specialists tend to highlight.

147

Because we humans tend to prize the competitive, destructive element over the egalitarian, cooperative one, we often end up discovering what we set out to find, alien behaviour that helps to validate our own ambivalent and convoluted value systems.

Thanks to recent discoveries in the anthropological and social sciences, we now realise that we were not always as barbaric and destructive as we are today. For much of our prehistoric existence we lived in closer harmony with the earth and with each other, *interconnected* with a sense of divine indwelling whereby we treated all life in a much more benevolent and ethical manner. The emerging evidence suggests that our current alienation and destructibility is largely the result of our attempts to conquer and control the earth within the unfolding Agricultural Revolution of the past 10,000 years.

Prior to that time a distinctly different quality of spirituality prevailed, with a much more coherent capacity to integrate the forces of light and darkness. Proportionately, people acted out of a much more enlightened person-planet ambience than we do today. And as we reconnect afresh with those deep layers of our collective story, the will-to-meaning awakens a new sense of spiritual engagement, unique to the times in which we live.

Many people make the initial connection in the human search for *meaning* in life. And some quickly realise that this is only possible when we learn to *relate* meaningfully: with self, others, creation and God. And then comes the significant leap – of heart and imagination – the conviction that it is well nigh impossible to have meaningful personal or interpersonal relationships without a meaningful planet in which to articulate and negotiate our capacity to relate. At this juncture, *justice* (what the Scriptures describe as 'righteousness') becomes a perennial concern.

It is this *power to connect*, more than anything else, that authenticates contemporary spirituality. It is a distinctively eclectic development, seeking a *depth* that goes far deeper into the sacred traditions than any religion, or even all the religions together, can facilitate; seeking a *breadth* that includes the whole of creation in its evolutionary unfolding; seeking an *integration* to move us beyond the dualisms of patriarchal fragmentation which has carved up our planet and alienated humans from each other and from the rest of creation; seeking a *transcendence* that does not seek to escape from, or overcome, the world, but transform it in a collaborative endeavour with our co-creative God.

Nothing less than this revitalised spiritual vision will satisfy those called to be a liminal presence in our world today, nor will anything less be capable of empowering us for the radical and creative witness required by our prophetic contestation. We don't need to be the robust, ascetical heroes of bygone days, but rather vulnerable, enlightened and earthy mystics, who are at home with dirty hands, fiery guts and wild imaginations. After two thousand years of Christianity it is about time we once more 'cast fire on the earth' and bring *incarnation* fully to life!

Connecting in Prayer

While visionaries like Christopher Fry assert that 'The human heart can go the length of God', religious gurus from various faith traditions have rarely shared that spiritual optimism. The spiritual tradition of the past few thousand years, even in an *incarnational* faith like Christianity, has often left us in a state of spiritual paralysis. God was frequently depicted as being so perfect, holy and complete, and we humans so imperfect, sinful and deranged that prayer became a type of infantile neurosis in which the naughty child forever tried , but rarely succeeded in pacifying the kind but insatiable parent-figure – classically depicted as a male, judgemental Lord. Little wonder, that prayer, even today, continues to be problematic for many people.

While the best in our tradition emphasised that prayer is, above all else, a *relationship* with a God of unconditional love, unconsciously we often reduced that relationship to the interpersonal realm; in other words, into an manageable anthropocentric package. In many cases, this led to another type of *dis*-connectedness, especially from the planetary and cosmic dimensions of our lives. And frequently it begot a false (or inadequate) sense of God, also disconnected from, or pitched over against, God's own creation from which every life-form emanates. The prayer of disconnectedness must now give way to a spirituality of connection which requires a fresh understanding of all spiritual expressions including that of prayer itself.

In fact, what we are about, largely unawares, is a rediscovery of very ancient modes of prayer, including a sense of awe and wonder around the mystery of life itself – experienced both benevolently and painfully. This is essentially what *meditation* is about, whether understood as a mystical prayer or the prayer of contemplation. It is in the words of Joan Chittister (already quoted in Chapter Two): '. . . the ability to see through, to see into, to see despite, to see without blindness. It is the ability to see a whole world rather than a partial one.'

The call to contemplation is not, and never was intended to be, the reserve for monks or recluses. It is a desire and capacity that arises in every human heart and yearns for expression and articulation. It arises as all prayer does through the power of the creative Spirit who prays within us (cf. Rom 8:26-27). Prayer is not something *we* do or achieve – alone or with others. Rather it is something that happens to us as our whole selves (body, mind and spirit) become porous and receptive to the creative power of God's Spirit at work in the whole of creation.

Prayer is a disposition of heart, not a skill bestowed from outside, rather a yearning and longing awakening from within. The 'withinness' always remains foundational and becomes the well-spring to forge connections and relationships. The forms, structures and even words arise as we need to formalise the stirrings of the heart. The words we use in prayer, the degree to which we attend or fail to attend to the words (distractions), is relatively unimportant. The intention and desire to be disposed to God in prayer is far more important than any humanly-construed exercise of prayer.

We also need to reclaim the social and communal dimensions of prayer. If prayer is a power-towards-connection then the context of a supportive and discerning group seems highly desirable. The group context is particularly important to engender a climate for discernment. Among other things this includes:

a. a capacity for deep listening;
b. a readiness to dialogue with vulnerability and darkness – with one self and others;
c. a transparency that is open to seek and search from within the collective wisdom of the group;
d. a readiness to move towards 'prayerful' action in the name of justice and gospel liberation;
e. creative ritualisation of significant experiences.

Like the spiritual capacity itself, the desire to pray is innate and spontaneous. It is the fragmentation and spiritual erosion of the past few thousand years that has jeopardised and undermined this rich, God-given resource. As we find ourselves pushed into a deepening consciousness of our interdependence as a human and planetary species, a re-awakening of prayer and spiritual connectedness is likely to become a global issue of enormous significance. It will mark a coming home to who we really are in our personal and planetary identity. It will be the rediscovery of *meaning*, largely subverted amid the religiosity of the past few thousand years.

Thank God our time is now...

This is yet another refounding moment for religious of our time. Can we bring ourselves to the cutting edge of this new shift in spiritual evolution? Can we be truly present in the liminal space that calls forth this new spiritual ferment? Can we engage with its challenge to transcend the 'value-free' (or value-less) confusion into which our world has been plunged? And finally, can we move to the prophetic horizons where those who hunger spiritually tell their story, loaded though it may be at times with ambiguity and contradiction?

Thank God our time is now:
- A time when the limited and limiting boundaries of spirit-awakening are being stretched to the inclusive horizons of God's New Reign;
- A time when we are called to transcend the dualisms of separation and fragmentation and reclaim the essential oneness of all life under God.
- A time to outgrow our national, ethnic, racist and religious distinctions as we reconnect with that spiritual ferment which must never be reduced to human categories no matter how sanctioned by time or culture;
- A time for creative re-balancing whereby we learn to befriend once more the daring and liberating creativity of the feminine, the imagination, the artist and the prophet;
- A time for depth to see anew and dream afresh beyond the superficial, utilitarian and sectarian impositions, often validated by formal religion to justify imperialists who exploit the poor and suffering of our earth;
- A time for incarnating our spiritual creativity to alter those systems and structures which undermine human dignity and planetary integrity, and to foster a just and equitable distribution of all our God-given resources. This requires a fresh and daring interaction between spirituality and our political systems.
- A time for the liberating use of rite and ritual to ground and incarnate our mutual responsibility for the growth and development of all God's creatures (planet Earth

included), and to facilitate a more widespread use of discerning and contemplative wisdom;

- Finally, a time for those called to the vowed life to be the courageous and generous catalysts for this new spiritual ferment, so that it does not become entrapped in religious fundamentalism, scientific reductionism or political secularism.

What we, religious, make of this time may have enormous consequences not merely for the future of the vowed life, or the Christian faith, but for human and planetary civilisation itself. Our liminal and prophetic call is to nothing less than this global engagement. Therein, also we stand the best chance of engaging cogently and creatively with the living Spirit of God in whose dying and being born anew we, too, are challenged to stand at new thresholds, beyond the Calvary of our dying mechanistic world, as we move towards the horizons of Resurrection possibility in a world in travail yearning to be born anew.

Our daily prayer needs to be for the wisdom and courage to outgrow our cherished past and embrace the new spiritual horizon that dawns on our world today. We need to pray for wisdom and courage, to engage the impending darkness, but more importantly, to reflect the light of hope that endures, and ultimately transforms – even our darkest hours.

Notes

1. Arbuckle (1988) quite rightly situates the renewal (refounding) of religious life in the context of the contemporary chaos, confusion and disintegration that characterise the modern world. The metaphor of *chaos* evokes powerful, primal images around the original chaos of creation itself (Gen 1:1ff), along with the disintegration and disillusionment of every death-resurrection experience. Contemporary scientists – and an increasing number of economists – employ the same metaphor, not merely to name the disintegration, but also to highlight the *order* and creative *possibilities* engendered from within, or because of, the chaos they perceive. (Cf. James Gleick, *Chaos*, Heinemann Books, 1988; Roger Lewin, *Complexity: Life at the Edge of Chaos*, London: J.M. Dent, 1993).

    To read the signs of the times today, to critique in a truly prophetic way what is going on in our world, religious need to engage with the volatile upsurges which characterise our times. To choose not to do so, because of a traditional anti-world stance, is a betrayal of our fundamental calling.

2. The idea was initially proposed by St Jerome and St Gregory the Great and revived in our own time by W.F. Albright, *The Biblical Period from Abraham to Ezra*, Harper & Row, 1963, p. 44. The analogy is developed at some length by Francis J. Moloney, *Disciples and Prophets: A Biblical Model for religious life*, London: Darton, Longman & Todd, 1980, pp. 155-170.

3. I borrow the term *value-radiation* (and later *value-radiation centre*) from the seminal, yet largely unknown, work of Adrian Van Kaam (1968). In Van Kaam's original usage the term is applied to each of the three vows, encapsulating a set of primordial (archetypal) values, shared by humans on an universal scale, but also belonging to the biopsychological structure of the animal kingdom (Van Kaam, pp. 12ff). In the present work, the term has a range of applications, the chief one being to the vowed life itself as the carrier of liminal and prophetic values on behalf of the wider culture.

4. Many argue that this is precisely the function of religion (*religio* means to link back to the origin). However, religion itself has become heavily institutionalised and, consequently, has become domesticated and conformed by the mainstream culture to such an extent that it has been largely divested of its capacity to serve in a counter-cultural context.

5. *Patriarchy* is a term used frequently in the present work to denote the social organisation of culture into systems that are hierarchical and male-dominated in terms of value and power. Male perceptions, interpretations, experiences, needs and interests predominate, sometimes promoted by women as well as by men. We consider patriarchy to have arisen concurrently with the Agricultural Revolution, originating around 8,000 BCE and prevailing until our own time.

6. An oft-cited work of Peter Brown on 'The Rise and Function of the Holy Man in Late Antiquity', in *Journal of Roman Studies*, 51 (1971), pp. 80-101, has many parallels with the notion of liminality, although the word is never used; also Jean Leclercq's notion of the fringe as a basic phenomenon in the monastic life developed in 'Monasticism and One World', *Cistercian Studies*, 21 (1986), pp. 277-310. Finally, there are some pertinent insights in Duncan Fisher, 'Liminality: The Vocation of the Church', *Cistercian Studies*, 24 (1989), pp. 181-205; 25 (1990), pp. 188-218.

7. Take, for example, the inconsistencies in recent Catholic teaching. In the documents of the Second Vatican Council, Church and Kingdom tend to be equated in *Lumen Gentium* (although the notion of Church as *the people of God* is quite a new development) whereas in *Gaudium et Spes* (39, 45) the Kingdom has priority over the Church. In the encyclical letter *Redemptoris Missio* (1990), the priority of the Kingdom is clearly and categorically affirmed (Nos. 12-20). Yet, a few years later, the New Universal Catechism (1993) tends to equate the two realities (see Nos. 541, 670-671, 732, 763, 768-769, 865). Little wonder, then, that the Church's own credibility is so much under question.

8. The tendency in patriarchal culture to undermine and underestimate female presence and feminine values, along with the use of religion to validate that oppression, is documented extensively in feminist literature. Although they are often considered to be extreme and exaggerated, I find the writings of Mary Daly to be most insightful and comprehensive on this subject. Her outstanding works include: *Beyond God the Father* (1973), *Gyn/Ecology: Toward a Metaethics of Feminism* (1978) and *Pure Lust: Elemental Feminist Philosophy* (1984), all published by Beacon Press, Boston.

9. According to Ignatius of Antioch and Clement of Alexandria, the public profession of virginity was recognised in the Church from the beginning of the second century. From the beginning of the third century, Tertullian and Cyprian allude to several virgins in the church of North Africa. Despite restrictions imposed by the Councils of Elvira (c. 306) and Ancyra (314), virgins in the East were supported enthusiastically by John Chrysostom, Gregory of Nazianzus, Gregory of Nyssa, Athanasius and Basil, and in the West by Ambrose and Jerome in particular.

10. Systems theory is one application of the scientific principle that the whole is greater than the sum of its constituent parts. It invites us to consider each system, organisation or group as an organism in its own right, with a 'life' of its own apart from its constituent parts. An awareness of systems theory is essential to appreciate fully the complex dynamics on which all groups – religious ones included – operate. More on this topic in James Miller, *Living Systems*, McGraw-Hill, 1978.

11. For example in the Gulf War (1990-1991), scud missiles (with their unmistakable phallic symbolism), when they missed their intended targets – usually cities on hilltops – tended to land in vulva-type valleys. Pure chance or a cultural acting-out of sexual oppression? (More on this topic in D.E.H. Russell, *Exposing Nuclear Phallacies*, Pergamon Press, 1989, especially pp. 54-59, 79, 133-141).

12. In this section I use the terms *ecclesiastical* and *ecclesial* interchangeably, although I acknowledge that the latter has a much wider frame of reference than the former. I understand the term *ecclesial* to refer to all those who comprise the Christian family by virtue of baptism, and *ecclesiastical* to denote the formal structures of sacrament and institution (particularly the latter) within which people formally live out their ecclesial identity.

13. As indicated previously, I am not suggesting that religious life has a monopoly over the gift of liminality. History seems to suggest that it is activated and mediated primarily, but not exclusively, through religious. The Church itself embodies liminal experience and can reflect liminal values as Starkloff (1997) clearly indicates. Many of Starkloff's reflections, however, refer to the *conscious* level of mediation; he seems to be largely unaware of the subconscious, cultural factors explored throughout the present work.

Bibliography

Anderson, B.S. and Zinsser, J.P. (1988), *A History of Their Own: Europe from Prehistory to the Present*, Viking/Penguin (2 Vols.).

Arbuckle, Gerald A. (1986), *Strategies for Growth in Religious Life*, St Paul Publications, Slough.

(1988), *Out of Chaos: Refounding Religious Congregations*, Paulist Press/Chapman.

(1993), *Refounding the Church*, Chapman.

Balducelli, Roger (1975), 'The Decision for Celibacy', *Theological Studies*, 36, pp. 653-668.

Barker, Eileen (1982), *New Religious Movements*, New York: Melen Press.

Barr, Kevin J. (1995), *Fire on the Earth: Prophetic Religious Life for the 21st. century*, Melbourne: Spectrum Publications.

Bausch, William (1975), *Positioning Belief in the Mid-Seventies*, Indiana: Fides Books.

Beckford, James (1986), *New Religious Movements and Rapid Social Change*, New Dehli: Sage Publications.

Billy, Denis J. (1993), *Evangelical Kernels: A Theological Spirituality of the Religious Life*, Alba House.

Boff, Leonardo (1986), *Ecclesiogenesis*, Westminster Press.

Brown, Raymond (1979), *The Community of the Beloved Disciple*, London: Chapman.

Bruns, J. Edgar (1973), *God as Woman, Woman as God*, Paulist Press.

Brueggemann, Walter (1978), *The Prophetic Imagination*, Fortress Press.

(1986), *The Hopeful Imagination*, Fortress Press.

Bynum, Caroline W. (1975) 'The Cistercian Conception of Community: An Aspect of Twelfth Century Spirituality', *Harvard Theological Review*, Vol. 69, pp. 273-286.

Cada, L. and Alia (1979), *Shaping the Coming Age of Religious Life*, Seabury Press.

Chitty, Derwas J. (1966), *The Desert a City*, Oxford: Blackwell.

(1975), *The Letters of St Anthony*, Oxford: SLG Press.

Chittister, Joan D. (1990), *Womanstrength*, Sheed & Ward.

(1994), 'Religious Life: Prophetic Dimension', *Religious Life Review*, 33, pp. 102-111.

(1995), *The Fire in These Ashes: A Spirituality of Contemporary Religious Life*, Kansas City: Sheed & Ward.

Conlon, James (1990), *Geo-Justice*, San Jose (CA): Resource Publications Inc.

Desprez, Vincent (1990), 'The Roots of Christian Monasticism: The Jewish Bible and Ancient Religions', *American Benedictine Review*, 41, pp. 348-356.

Drucker, Peter (1989), *The New Realities*, Harper & Row.

Eisler, Raine (1987), *The Chalice and the Blade*, Pandora Books.
(1995), *Sacred Pleasure: Sex, Myth and the Politics of the Body*, New
York: HarperCollins; Shaftesbury (Dorset): Element Books.

Eliade, Mircea (1964), *Shamanism: Archaic Techniques of Ecstasy*, Pan-
theon Books.

Estes, Clarissa Pinkola (1992), *Women Who Run With the Wolves*, Rider
Publications.

Evola, Julius (1983), *The Metaphysics of Sex*, London: East-West Publications.

Falk, Nancy E. (1987), 'Feminine Sacrality', *The Encyclopaedia of Religion*, vol. 5 (pp. 302-312), MacMillan & Free Press.

Fedwick, Paul (1979), *The Church and the Charisma of Leadership in Basil
of Caesarea*, Toronto: Pontifical Institute of Mediaeval Studies.

Ferguson, Marilyn (1982), *The Aquarian Conspiracy: Personal and Social
Transformation in the 1980s*, Tarcher/ Routledge & Kegan Paul.

Fiand, Barbara (1987), *Releasement: Spirituality for Ministry*, Crossroad.
(1990), *Living the Vision*, Crossroad.
(1992), *Where Two or Three are Gathered*, Crossroad.
(1996), *Wrestling with God: Religious Life in Search of its Soul*, New
York: Crossroad

Fisher, Duncan (1989, 1990), 'Liminality: The Vocation of the Church',
Cistercian Studies, 24 (pp. 181-205), 25 (pp.188- 218).

Fox, Matthew (1994), *The Reinvention of Work*, Harper.

Frend, W.H.C. (1965), *Martyrdom and Persecution in the Early Church*,
Oxford: Blackwell.

Fuellenbach, John (1995), *The Kingdom of God*, Maryknoll (NY): Orbis
Books.

Greenstein, George (1988), *The Symbiotic Universe*, New York: William
Morrow & Co.

Gribomont, Jean (1965), 'Le Monachisme un Sein de l'Eglise en Syrie et en
Cappodoce', *Studia Monastica*, 7, pp. 7-24.

Henry, P.G. and Swearer, D.K. (1989), *For the Sake of the World: The
Spirit of Buddhist and Christian Monasticism*, Fortress Press/The Liturgical Press.

Heschel, Abraham (1960), *The Prophets*, Harper & Row.

Hobbs, T.R. (1985), 'The Search for Prophetic Consciousness', *Biblical
Theology Bulletin*, 15, pp. 136-141

hooks, bell (1991), *Yearning: Race, Gender and Cultural Politics*, Boston:
South End Press.

Hostie, Raymond (1972), *Vie et Mort des Ordres Religieux*, Desclee de
Brower.

John Paul II, Pope (1996), *Vita Consecrata: The Consecrated Life and its
Mission in the Church and the World*, London: Catholic Truth Society.

Johnson, Elizabeth A. (1994), 'Between the Times: Religious Life and the
Postmodern Experience of God', *Review for Religious*, 53, pp. 6-28.

Jung, C.G. (1968), *Man and His Symbols*, New York: Dell.

Kittel, Gerhard (1964), 'Eremos (Desert)' in *Theological Dictionary of the New Testament*, W.B. Eerdmans, Vol. 2, pp. 657-659.
Knitter, Paul F. (1995), *One Earth, Many Religions*, Maryknoll (NY): Orbis Books.

Larrington, Carolyne, ed. (1992), *The Feminist Companion to Mythology*, Harper Collins.
Lawlor, Robert (1989), *Earth Honoring: The New Male Sexuality*, Rochester (VT): Park St. Press.
Leakey, Richard E. (1992), *Origins Reconsidered: In Search of What Makes Us Human*, Abacus Books.
Leddy, Mary Jo (1990), *Reweaving Religious Life*, Mystic (Conn.): Twenty-Third Publications.
Lee, Bernard J. (1989), 'A Socio-Historical Theology of Charism', *Review for Religious*, 48, pp. 124-135.
Leroi-Gourhan, André (1968), 'The Evolution of Paleolithic Art', *Scientific American*, Vol. 218, pp. 58-70.
Lovelock, James (1979), *Gaia: A New Look at Life on Earth*; (1988), *The Ages of Gaia*, both published by Oxford University Press (Oxford and New York).

Malone, Edward E. (1950), *The Monk and the Martyr*, Washington: Catholic University of America Press.
McFague, Sallie (1993), *The Body of God: An Ecological Theology*, London: SCM Press.
McNamara, Jo Ann Kay (1996), *Sisters in Arms: Catholic Nuns Through Two Millennia*, Cambridge (MASS) and London: Harvard University Press.
Merkle, Judith A. (1992), *Committed By Choice: Religious Life Today*, Collegeville (Minn.): The Liturgical Press.
Metz, Johannes (1978), *Followers of Christ*, Burns & Oates
Meyer, M.W. and Zucker, L.G. (1989), *Permanently Failing Organisations*, Sage Publications.
Murray, Robert (1974), 'The Exhortation to Candidates for Ascetical Vows at Baptism in the Ancient Syrian Church', *New Testament Studies*, 21, pp. 59-79.

Nedungatt, G. (1973), 'The Covenanters of the Early Syriac-speaking Church', *Orientalia Christiana Periodica*, 39, pp. , 191-215; 419-444.
Nelson, James B. & Longfellow, Sandra P., Eds, (1994), *Sexuality and the Sacred*, London: Mowbray; Louisville (KY):Westminster/John Knox Press.

O'Murchu, Diarmuid (1991), *Religious Life: A Prophetic Vision*, Indiana: Ave Maria Press / London: Excalibur Press.
(1996), *Quantum Theology*, New York: Crossroad.
(1997), *Reclaiming Spirituality*, Dublin: Gill & Macmillan; New York: Crossroad.

Raphael, Melissa (1996), *Thealogy and Embodiment*, Sheffield: Sheffield Academic Press.

Reuther, Rosemary Radford (1992), *Gaia and God*, Crossroad.

Sahtouris, Elizabet (1989), *Gaia: The Human Journey from Chaos to Cosmos*, London, New York, Sydney: Pocket Books.

Schneiders, Sandra (1986), *New Wineskins: Re-imaging Religious Life Today*, Paulist Press.

Sheehan, Thomas (1986), *The First Coming: How the Kingdom of God Became Christianity*, Random House.

Sieveking, Ann (1983), 'Palaeolithic Art', in Lawrence Gowing (ed.), *A History of Art*, MacMillan, pp. 2-10.

Singer, June (1977), *Androgyny: Toward a New Theory of Sexuality*, Anchor Books.

Sjoo, Monica and Mor, Barbara (1987), *The Great Cosmic Mother*, San Francisco: Harper.

Southern, R.W. (1970), *Western Society and the Church in the Middle Ages*, Penguin Books.

Starkloff, Carl F. (1997), 'Church as Structure and Communitas: Victor Turner and Ecclesiology,' *Theological Studies*, 58 (1997), 643-668.

Stone, Merlin (1976), *When God Was a Woman*, New York: Harcourt Brace Jovanovich.

Swimme, Brian and Berry, Thomas (1992), *The Universe Story*, Harper & Row.

Trimingham, J.S. (1971), *The Sufi Orders in Islam*, Oxford: Clarendon Press.

Tsomo, Karma Lekshe (1988), *Sakyadhita: Daughters of the Buddha*, New York: Snow Lion Publications.

Turner, Victor and Edith (1969), *The Ritual Process: Structure and Anti-Structure*, Chicago: Aldine.

(1974), *Dramas, Fields and Metaphors*, Cornell University Press.

(1978), *Image and Pilgrimage in Christian Culture*, Oxford: Blackwell.

(1985), 'Liminality, Kabbalah and Media', *Religion*, 15, pp. 205-217.

Van Kaam, Adrian (1968), *The Vowed Life*, Dimension Books.

Waltzlawick, P., Weakland, J. and Fisch, R. (1974), *Change: Principles of Problem Formation and Problem Resolution,* New York: Norton.

Wilson Schaef, Anne (1987), *When Society Becomes an Addict*, Harper & Row.

Wittberg, Patricia (1991), *Creating a Future for Religious Life*, Paulist Press.

Zappone, Katherine (1991), *The Hope for Wholeness*, Mystic (Conn.): Twenty-Third Publications.